P9-AFX-721

Priests for a New Millennium

A SERIES OF

ESSAYS ON THE

MINISTERIAL PRIESTHOOD

BY THE CATHOLIC BISHOPS OF

THE UNITED STATES

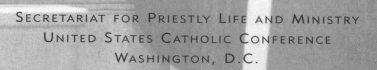

SECRETARIAT FOR PRIESTLY LIFE AND MINISTRY
UNITED STATES CATHOLIC CONFERENCE
WASHINGTON, D.C.

Priests for a New Millennium, a collection of reflections on the priesthood by U.S. Catholic bishops, was a project of the Secretariat for Priestly Life and Ministry. The content was solicited and shaped by an editorial board led by Bishop Richard C. Hanifen, chairman of the Bishops' Committee on Priestly Life and Ministry. The resulting collection of essays is authorized for publication by the undersigned.

Monsignor Dennis M. Schnurr
General Secretary, NCCB/USCC

The address by Archbishop Gabriel Montalvo, apostolic nuncio, was originally delivered at the November 1999 general meeting of bishops. The text and citations are reprinted, with permission, in their entirety.

Excerpts from the English translation of the *Catechism of the Catholic Church* for the United States of America copyright © 1994, United States Catholic Conference, Inc.-Libreria Editrice Vaticana. English translation of the *Catechism of the Catholic Church: Modifications from the Editio Typica* copyright © 1997, United States Catholic Conference, Inc.-Libreria Editrice Vaticana. Used with permission. All rights reserved.

Scripture texts used in this work are taken from the *New American Bible*, copyright © 1991, 1986, and 1970 by the Confraternity of Christian Doctrine, Washington, DC 20017 and are used by permission of the copyright owner. All rights reserved.

Excerpts from *Vatican Council II: The Conciliar and Post Conciliar Documents* edited by Austin Flannery, OP, copyright © 1975, Costello Publishing Company, Inc., Northport, N.Y. are used with permission of the publisher, all rights reserved. No part of these excerpts may be reproduced, stored in a retrieval system, or transmitted in any form or by any means—electronic, mechanical, photocopying, recording, or otherwise—without express written permission of Costello Publishing Company.

Excerpts from *The Documents of Vatican II*, Walter M. Abbott, SJ, General Editor, copyright © 1966 by America Press, Inc. Reprinted with permission. All rights reserved.

First Printing, November 2000

ISBN 1-57455-367-4

Contents

ADDRESS OF HIS EXCELLENCY ARCHBISHOP GABRIEL MONTALVO, APOSTOLIC NUNCIO

General Meeting of the U.S. Catholic Bishops
November 15, 1999

In his address to the full assembly of bishops at their autumn 1999 meeting, Archbishop Montalvo discussed the identity and mission of the priesthood and called for the bishops to respond in their own relationships with their priests. The following collection of essays was developed in the same spirit. We are pleased to print the papal nuncio's address.

1. Once again it was with great joy that I welcomed your gracious invitation to offer this presentation before the plenary session of the National Conference of Catholic Bishops of the United States of America. First, I should like to express my gratitude to his excellency Bishop Joseph Fiorenza, your president, for the honor and privilege of sharing a word with each and every one of you, dear bishops. In the name of the Holy Father, I extend a heartfelt greeting and many good wishes that the work of these days might not only be pleasant and productive, but most of all that it be rich, bearing abundant fruit for the life and the work of the whole Church in this great and wonderful country.

2. The topics forming the agenda of your meeting are many and certainly of no little importance. The Holy See and the Holy Father himself faithfully follow your deliberations with a hope that the decisions and outcomes might contribute to an even stronger ecclesial communion: a communion which not only unites all of you with the vicar of Christ, but which is also at the heart of your episcopal body and central to your ministries in your dioceses. This very "communion" with the pope and among yourselves, the fact that you are successors to the apostles, is the essential element upon which your leadership is based in each of the dioceses that are entrusted to your pastoral care.

3. By the grace of God, the Church in the United States enjoys a great vitality that is manifested in various ways. Presently, in this country we are seeing significant numbers of people being consecrated to God and the emergence of new apostolates; each of them requires a greater attention on the part of the bishops, so that by their prudent and vigilant direction these faithful sons and daughters might receive their just place in the Church. If it is true, and it is, that *ubi Petrus ibi ecclesia*, then, by analogy, every initiative and activity within the diocese must necessarily refer to the bishop of that diocese. Therefore, one can hardly imagine a situation in which the magisterial or pastoral action of the bishop could be considered an illicit or inappropriate interference.

4. By the will of Christ and by the very nature of things, there are in the Church and in the dioceses some realities which have always existed and without which it would not even be possible to conceive of ecclesiastical life itself. Even these realities, obviously, refer to the bishops. Reflecting "on the opportunities presented by the great jubilee for evangelization in the light of the extraordinary grace which was and is the Second Vatican Council and on the importance for the spiritual renewal of the Christian community," the Holy Father, in addressing the bishops of the provinces of Detroit and

Cincinnati, called their attention to the identity and the mission of priests as "your co-workers in the task of sanctifying the people of God and handing on the faith" (*Lumen Gentium*, no. 28).

5. In fact it is superfluous to point out that the priesthood is an essential element in the nature and life of the Church. While in many countries, particularly in Europe, one feels more and more the absence of vocations to the priesthood, in your country fortunately there still are steady numbers of candidates for holy orders. However, I think we can all agree that years ago most of the seminaries enrolled larger numbers of seminarians. The magnitude of this problem is augmented by the fact that the number of Catholics in this country is increasing as new populations are coming from Asia, Central and South America and even from some countries in Europe. These people need to receive spiritual assistance in ways that are ongoing and appropriate. The Holy Father often says, "A bishop cannot fail to be personally involved in the promotion of vocations to the priesthood, and he needs to encourage the whole community of faith to play an active role in this way. The time has come to speak courageously about priestly life as a priceless gift and a splendid and privileged form of Christian living" (*Pastores Dabo Vobis*, no. 39).

6. However, more important than the number is the quality of the priests, as well as the good and sound preparation that is offered to them in programs of priestly formation. In the above-mentioned discourse of the Holy Father to the bishops of the provinces of Detroit and Cincinnati, the pope, recalling with great joy the celebration of his golden jubilee of priestly ordination, said, among other things: "It is vital for the life of the church in your dioceses that you devote much attention to your priests and to the quality of their life and ministry. Through word and example you should constantly remind them that the priesthood is a special vocation which consists in being uniquely configured to Christ the high

priest, the teacher, sanctifier and shepherd of his people" (May 21-27, 1998, *L'Osservatore Romano*).

7. In these initial months of my residency here in the United States, I have already made several pleasant and varied journeys to dioceses throughout the country and I have had the impression that generally there are excellent relationships among you and your priests. You love and respect your priests, and they, in turn, respond with the same sentiments toward each of you. Without wishing to interfere in your pastoral ministry, permit me to invite you once again, in the name of the Holy Father, to always strive to have a greater understanding of your priests, to always be ready to listen to them and to support them. Be eager to help them when, particularly because of human weakness, they find themselves in difficult situations. Unfortunately, it is true that some priests have placed themselves in situations that are incompatible with their state in life. These, however, are cases that we could qualify as isolated. For this reason, I should like to recall the words of our Holy Father, "With immense gratitude I think of all your priests whose lives are deeply marked by fidelity to Christ and generous dedication to their brothers and sisters" (ibid.).

8. Priests must be able to look to their bishops to draw strength so that they might be faithful to their vocations, to be "truly effective witnesses to Christ and teachers of the faith. We have to be men of prayer like Christ himself. Priests and seminarians preparing for the priesthood need to interiorize the fact that there is an intimate bond between the priest's spiritual life and the exercise of his ministry" (*Pastores Dabo Vobis*, no. 24).

9. We all believe that the most important moment of our day is that time which is set apart for the celebration of the Eucharist, the very center of our lives. It is really through experience in dealing with young priests that I have no doubt in affirming that the daily

celebration of the Holy Mass is for us and for them the true font of fidelity to the Lord and to priestly responsibilities. One cannot emphasize this enough in the formation of future priests.

10. In speaking of the Eucharist, I am moved to reflect on the power and richness of the great sacrament of Reconciliation, which best disposes the human heart for every encounter with our Lord Jesus Christ. I do not want to make a negative comment; however, I would be less than sincere if I did not mention that I have the impression that more could be done to encourage the faithful to approach the sacrament of Reconciliation with greater frequency and regularity. Perhaps we priests and bishops are called to be even more faithful in seeking and receiving the forgiveness of our Lord, so that we might be even better disposed to administer this sacrament of God's mercy.

11. Last, speaking to you bishops, whose adhesion to the magisterium of the Church is and must be complete, I think it would be superfluous to touch upon the questions of a canonical nature which pertain to the priesthood. Therefore, I limit my remarks to recall, with Pope John Paul, that the priesthood is a gift and a mystery and that no individual can claim a "right" to be ordained a priest.

12. I look forward with great joy to welcoming each and every one of you at the nunciature this evening as we gather to share a meal in fraternal esteem and affection for each other. As you well know, the nunciature is the Holy Father's house here in the United States. In this sense, it is your home as well and you should always feel "at home" at the nunciature. It is my sincere hope that moments such as this will draw all of us—bishops and representatives at the nunciature—together in mutually supportive and enthusiastic relationships. Thank you.

INTRODUCTION

Most Reverend Richard Hanifen
Bishop of Colorado Springs
Chairman, Bishops' Committee on Priestly Life and Ministry

The Church in our country has been marked by tremendous growth, especially since the end of the Second Vatican Council. We have witnessed a growth in both the size and the diversity of our Catholic population. We have seen a marvelous increase in the number of Catholic lay women and men who have been called forth from our communities to serve in a variety of ministries. We have been encouraged by the great many who have embraced their baptismal commitment in order to assist in the transformation of our society. As we stand at the beginning of a new millennium, we are confident that our ecclesial community is strong and vibrant. Our mission to proclaim a new evangelization is needed more than ever. The summons to promote justice and peace draws us forward into the new millennium to meet the challenges of a new day.

As we look at this vibrant life and mission of our Church, and as we celebrate the involvement of all the baptized—especially an emerging corps of lay ecclesial ministers—we are also mindful of the essential place of our priests in all of this. We are aware that much has changed in the context in which priestly life and ministry are lived out today in the United States. This context is extraordinarily complex. Many of our people, even some of our priests, have a limited appreciation of the full theological understanding of many sacraments, but especially of Holy Orders. Some presbyterates are marked by division. In many dioceses, an incredible growth in the Catholic population and simultaneous decline in the number of priests have complicated the pastoral horizon. Certainly the service provided by a pastor today has become more complex. Social and economic developments, demographic shifts, and ecclesial tensions have created a climate that can be very challenging for priests trying to faithfully live out their vocations in service to God and to the Church. Yet despite the tensions and challenges, priests continue to do the work of the Lord, often in heroic ways.

His Excellency Archbishop Gabriel Montalvo, in his address to the 1999 General Meeting of the National Conference of Catholic Bishops, reminded the bishops of this country of the great words that Pope John Paul II wrote in his exhortation *Pastores Dabo Vobis*: "The time has come to speak courageously about priestly life as a priceless gift and a splendid and privileged form of Christian living" (no. 39). Indeed, the archbishop was right to remind us that this is the proper time to speak courageously about the priesthood.

The Lord continues to shepherd and nourish his people through the ministry and lives of priests. The ministry that priests offer is invaluable; when they allow the Holy Spirit to work through them, priests have an impact far beyond their numbers. This collection of essays is offered in the hope of encouraging, enlightening, nourishing, and strengthening priests so that they might be able to continue to respond to Christ's call to be nourishment for the people they serve.

A vast body of literature on the priesthood has been published since the close of the Second Vatican Council. As one historian has suggested, the time since the Council has been the "era of the scrutinized and studied priest." There have been surveys, studies, dissertations, and research papers. So why would we offer yet another book on a well-worn topic?

This book of essays is not a detached analysis of some aspect of the priesthood, written from a purely clinical or academic perspective. It is, rather, a collection of essays written by bishops for priests. Although the essays are not academic in nature, they do reflect the scholarship, pastoral experience, and wisdom of the bishops who wrote them. We are grateful to each of our writers: Archbishop Gabriel Montalvo, the Apostolic Nuncio; Bishop John D'Arcy, of Fort Wayne-South Bend; Archbishop Daniel Buechlein, of Indianapolis; Bishop Robert Lynch, of St. Petersburg; Francis Cardinal George, of Chicago; Archbishop Charles Chaput, of Denver; Roger Cardinal Mahony, of Los Angeles; Bishop Donald Wuerl, of Pittsburgh; Bishop Howard Hubbard, of Albany; Bishop William Skylstad, of Spokane; Bishop Blase Cupich, of Rapid City; Bishop Gerald Barnes, of San Bernardino; and Bishop Paul Loverde, of Arlington. While the style and theme developed by each writer is unique to each, what the reader will find in each essay is genuine wisdom and insight into the life and ministry of priests, as well as an abiding affection and esteem for those with whom they have shared the sacred bond of priesthood.

Thanks are also due to our editorial board: Rev. Augustine DiNoia, OP, of the Secretariat for Doctrine and Pastoral Practices; Rev. Thomas Mullen, SSL, of St. Charles Borromeo Seminary and the Archdiocese of Philadelphia; Rev. Bartholomew Winters, STD, of Mundelein Seminary and the Archdiocese of Chicago; and finally our managing editor, Rev. J. Cletus Kiley, executive director of the Secretariat for Priestly Life and Ministry.

Our hope is that these essays will be read by our priests and bishops and will be shared with our seminarians, with those currently engaged in lay ecclesial ministry, with those in formation, and finally, with our people who again and again express their care and desire for priests in their midst. These essays are offered in a spirit of love for the Church and for the priests whose lives and ministries have so richly blessed it.

Sincerely Yours in Christ,

+ Richard C. Hanifen

Most Reverend Richard Hanifen, DD
Bishop of Colorado Springs
Chairman, Bishops' Committee on
Priestly Life and Ministry

BISHOPS' COMMITTEE ON PRIESTLY LIFE AND MINISTRY

Bishop Francis J. Christian
Auxiliary Bishop of Manchester

Bishop William S. Skylstad
Bishop of Spokane

Bishop John R. Gaydos
Bishop of Jefferson City

Bishop Arthur N. Tafoya
Bishop of Pueblo

Bishop George H. Niederauer
Bishop of Salt Lake City

Bishop Paul A. Zipfel
Bishop of Bismarck

STAFF

Rev. J. Cletus Kiley
Executive Director, Secretariat for Priestly Life and Ministry

CONSULTANTS

Very Rev. Frederick P. Annie

Msgr. Timothy Dyer

Very Rev. Robert F. Guay

Rev. William D. Hammer

Rev. Charles Latus

Rev. Frank Reale, SJ

Rev. Kevin J. Spiess

Rev. Francis S. Tebbe, OFM

Rev. Don Wolf

THE CALL TO COMMUNION AND THE ROAD TO PRIESTLY MATURITY: "CIRCLES OF COMMUNION"

Most Reverend John M. D'Arcy
Bishop of Fort Wayne-South Bend

I believe there has never been a time in the history of the Church when there has been so much material on priestly identity: rich material, rooted in the mystery of the Trinity and the nature of the Church. It seems that many of the truths of the Second Vatican Council, which our Holy Father calls "providential," are now, at last, coming more fully into the life of the Church. These truths have been examined and enriched by the international synods, especially the extraordinary Synod of 1986 and, central to our reflection, the Synod on Priestly Formation of 1990, after which Pope John Paul II issued *Pastores Dabo Vobis*.[1] Is this not part of what the pope refers to when he expects, across the threshold of the new millennium, "that new springtime of Christian life which will be revealed by the Great Jubilee, if Christians are docile to the action of the Holy Spirit"?[2]

On the matter of priestly identity, the Holy Thursday letters of Pope John Paul II, along with his talks to priests during his pastoral visits on "the roadways of the world," as he himself would say, have developed and applied the Council's teaching on priestly identity, linking it always with the priesthood of Christ and the priesthood as shared by all the baptized. Especially helpful is his talk given to priests in Philadelphia on his first pastoral visit to this country. In *Pastores Dabo Vobis* as well, we find a compendium of the dogmatic and spiritual theology of the priesthood.

Those involved in the ministry of priestly formation today, whether in seminaries or among those who work with ordained priests, recognize that the key to a renewed ministerial priesthood is the ever more complete acceptance of a true priestly identity. Yet in saying this, I have said very little, or at least I have not said enough. I am convinced that there are obstacles in most of our lives that must be addressed and overcome if the magnificent concepts of priestly identity that are being presented to us by the Church are to be internalized and become the driving force in our lives.

About this internalization—this integration of the profound truths being presented to us by the Church—not enough has been written. Even among the apostles themselves, we find ambition, jealousy, and fear, and we see that the Lord needed to give them spiritual guidance, helping them to face these weaknesses. This guidance was provided before the Last Supper and before Pentecost. Commitment to be lasting and fruitful must be accompanied by spiritual and emotional growth. It cannot precede it; or if it does precede it, the commitment is unlikely to last. Recent decades have shown this all too clearly and painfully.

Thus, the questions presented by the episcopal committee for my consideration appear to be especially pertinent and to demand a response that is not superficial:

- As we look to the new millennium, how can we help priests understand and interiorize this profoundly spiritual and theological foundation of their identity?
- How can we help them to draw out the implications of this identity for their ministry and mission?

I share these convictions after serving for forty-three years as a priest and fifteen years as a spiritual director in a major seminary, after preaching more than fifty retreats to priests and bishops, and while living my twenty-fifth year as a bishop and fifteenth as pastor of one diocese—married to that diocese, as the fathers of the Church would have it. How can I ever thank God sufficiently for leading me on such a road? Even a slow learner like myself should have acquired a bit of wisdom after such experience.

WHAT ARE THESE TRUTHS?

I select two truths that are deeply related to each other, as are all theological truths, and that are quite fully developed in *Pastores Dabo Vobis*. Let me repeat that the ever clearer emergence of these truths, so long held by the Church, does not in itself give sufficient promise for the renewal of the ministerial priesthood. That promise will be realized on an individual basis as priests and bishops, through the power of grace, accept the place these truths have in their own lives. This often involves struggle and never happens without grace. In fact, it is entirely a work of grace.

The first truth is often called "communion," referring to receiving and living out the intense love within the Holy Trinity. To grasp the conciliar and biblical root of this gift of intimacy with God, we should look to the first chapter of *Lumen Gentium* (*Dogmatic Constitution on the Church*). Here we see the biblical basis, deeply rooted in the New Testament, of this communion between Jesus Christ and the Church, and between Jesus Christ and each of his followers. The various biblical images, especially those connoting an internal and dynamic vitality (such as the Body, the Spouse, the Vine, and the Branches), bring home the close relationship that God seeks, that he has indeed accomplished through the sacrifice of Christ, and that has become a reality in the life of each person through Baptism. We also learn—and this is where spirituality comes in—that this communion is not just external. It is internal. It only comes to full fruition when it is accepted. This requires being open to divine grace.

The second truth, which relates closely to the priest's life, makes clear that the priest is a shepherd after the heart of Christ: "The priest's fundamental relationship is to Jesus Christ, Head and Shepherd."[3] To be aware of Christ's work as the Shepherd who lays down his life for the flock, and to sense that the priest's life is to be a shepherd after Christ's heart, is to realize that no one takes this office to himself. A personal call from Jesus Christ is required. In the Scriptures and in the lives of the saints, the acceptance of a personal call—a vocation—has often involved a time of struggle. Why should it be different for us?

A Man in Communion

This communion with the Divine Persons, given at Baptism, is transforming. We are "made over." The priest is likewise "made over" by the laying on of hands. This transformation is not something external: "It is not a question of 'relations' which are merely juxtaposed, but rather of ones which are interiorly united in a kind of mutual immanence."[4]

The Church's understanding of how the priest is "made over" and transformed is becoming ever clearer, but his acceptance of what has happened is the work of a lifetime:

> In the Church and on behalf of the Church, priests are a sacramental representation of Jesus Christ, the Head and Shepherd, authoritatively proclaiming his Word, repeating his acts of forgiveness and his offer of salvation, particularly in Baptism, Penance and the Eucharist, showing his loving concern to the point of a total gift of self for the flock, which they gather into unity and lead to the Father through Christ and in the Spirit. In a word, priests exist and act in order to proclaim the Gospel to the world and to build up the Church in the name and person of Christ the Head and Shepherd.[5]

Now this is all well enough for us to write out; but as I have said, there are obstacles to be overcome, and realities both human and divine to be faced, before the priest comes to full peace with what he has done with his life and before that peace begins to affect his life, enriching it from within. A priest needs both the theory and the practice. *Pastores Dabo Vobis* and other church documents beautifully lay out the theory on the relationship between the priest and Jesus Christ, and the priest's relationship, through Christ, to his bishop, to other priests, and to the people he serves. The priest is a man in communion. His communion with Christ and with his bishop is one. He shows the bishop's concern for the Church and works in union with his brother priests in a service of love for the flock and in promotion of the priesthood of the baptized. But from out of the events of his daily life, he must address this question: Is this communion really true, and does it apply to me? How does a priest come to believe it, to accept it as a central truth of his life—the light by which he walks and lives, the basis for his decisions? The rich theology of *Pastores Dabo Vobis* will not sustain him unless he faces a certain ultimate question: Has Jesus Christ really called me to be a priest? In the words of the Scriptures, am I "one of those he wanted"? "He went up the mountain and summoned those whom he wanted, and they came to him" (Mk 3:13). Another translation puts it this way: "He called to Himself those He had decided on." How can I come to that joyous belief that I am one of the ones he decided on?

Another question follows from the first: the question of the content of the priestly life. I could put it another way, linking it to the first question: "Wanted for what? Decided on for what?"

Consequences of Not Addressing These Issues

The priest who has failed to internalize the divine call as really coming from Christ (the first spiritual question), and the content and nature of the priestly vocation as seen by the Church (the second question, closely related to the first), will find himself caught in a web of spiritual and emotional insecurity. I am convinced that full acceptance of the call is one of the graces Christ wants most to give to priests because it is so essential for the growth of the Church; but I also believe that this acceptance is often resisted— not through any bad will, but through a kind of anxiety or fear about facing such questions. Such questions bring anxiety because they are so ultimate. But God himself is ultimate, and facing this question in a spirit of openness releases the love of the Trinity into our own lives and ministry.

In *Introduction to Christianity*, Joseph Cardinal Ratzinger gives us the striking example of Thérèse of Lisieux, a Doctor of the Church, who experienced the fear that all is darkness. Yet she continued to trust the light of God even though it seemed to her to be dimmed.[6] Faith and vocation are often under challenge. The challenges come from within us, as well as from the surrounding culture. Yet the challenges, if properly faced with openness to grace, bring about a stronger faith and a firmer vocational commitment.

Insecurity shows. It cannot be hidden. The priest who has not internalized and accepted the belief that he is one of the ones Jesus "wanted," and who has not pondered the question ("Wanted for what?") will find that insecurity will manifest itself in one of two ways. He will tend to become either clerical or anticlerical.

If clerical, he will be slow to foster the gifts of the laity, to call and welcome them into the apostolates or works to which Christ has called them. He will fail to discern those who are truly called to the ministry of the Church and those who are not. He will be afraid that his own place will be lost. Often this insecurity is not fully conscious, which makes it all the more harmful. Also, he will lack approachability, a willingness to listen. All the consultative bodies of parish life, still relatively new, will appear somewhat threatening to him. Failure to internalize his priesthood will make him either too submissive to his lay advisors or too authoritarian towards them. The priest's failure to accept fully the gift he has been given often will force him into a defensive stance. Yet there must never be a contradiction between the vocation of the lay person and that of the priest.

Or he will be guilty of anticlericalism: "I am no different from you. Call me Joe. I will even look like you and dress like you." I once met a priest who would not place the presider's chair within the sanctuary. I also saw this once in a religious house.

It is claimed that such a position for the celebrant is seen as separating the priest/celebrant too much from the laity. He is one of us after all. As priests, we are indeed one with the people, since we share with them the baptismal priesthood. But if we are no different, we have nothing to give them. In the divine plan, the priesthood of the laity will not flower without the full engagement of the priesthood of the ordained. The priest's chair placed in the sanctuary is a symbol not of power but of service. It reflects his identity as *in persona Christi Capitis*—in the Person of Christ the Head. As Head of the Body and as Shepherd, Christ is always active in the Church, giving life to the Body that is the Church and caring for the flock. But this must be made visible. We are a sacramental Church, going through the visible to the invisible. The priest makes this truth visible by his life as well as by what he does.

The ordained priest gives his life to build up the priesthood of the baptized in communion with his bishop and his brother priests. The priest, by his action and his life, embodies Christ, the Head and the Shepherd. The laity have an instinct about this; except for those who are bound by a contemporary ideology, they hunger for a priest who knows who he is, welcomes them as his coworkers, and strives to accept in his heart that he is not chosen by the community but, as Pope John Paul II puts it, is a gift of Christ to the community.[7]

Believing that Christ has called him and opening himself to the nature of the call do not separate the priest from the laity. Rather, the internalization and acceptance of both related truths bring him to peace, ease his insecurity, consecrate him to the service of the baptized, and draw him steadily to that spiritual vigor and fortitude that is central to priestly leadership and is so evident and attractive in the life of Pope John Paul II. The priest's ministry of word, sacrament, and pastoral care nourishes the life of faith of the flock, as well as their call to the lay apostolate and to the full understanding and exercise of their baptismal priesthood.

But many shy from this journey of vocational acceptance because it seems so threatening. Indeed, not setting out on this journey will prove to be the most threatening of all, because it brings about an insecurity that becomes evident to the people we serve and painful to ourselves.

THE NATURE OF THE JOURNEY AND SOME EXAMPLES

The root of this resistance to fully accepting the call of Christ resides in all of us. Even priests who have lived lives that can only be called innocent and pure sometimes find deep in themselves this anxiety for the authenticity of their call. This anxiety comes from a sense of unworthiness. It was experienced by Peter: "Depart from me, Lord, for I am a sinful man" (Lk 5:8). Indeed, such a cry from Peter and from all of us often represents the beginning of the full acceptance of the divine call: "Do not be afraid; from now on you will be catching men" (Lk 5:10). Conversation with the Lord about the call casts out fear. Let us look more closely at some of these fears.

Sometimes the priest or the seminarian, as he looks back over the causes that drew him to this life, fails to see that these causes are instruments of God, and he never breaks into the beautiful sunlight of a response that is more mature, more free, more deeply personal, and more rooted in the divine. An example may help. I once knew a priest with outstanding qualifications, although like many of us, he tended to be too hard on himself, never accepting his own beautiful goodness. He went away on a retreat experience—partly retreat and partly rest and relaxation. (The older I get, by the way, I think this is the best kind. Some retreats are just too intense.) He did a good deal of reading, and when he returned, he surprised me. The following are his words, exactly as I remember them:

> I think I've always been afraid that the reason I became a priest is to please my mother and father. But this is not true. A great deal of it is my own. Nevertheless, I must work to make it more my own.

In a time of prayer and grace, God showed him that a vocation is not something sheltered or held apart, enclosed in a tight package. If it is to grow, it must be opened, examined, and submitted to the dual light of reason and grace. Then the instruments—such as parents, other priests, or friends—can be seen as what they really are: God's instruments in drawing the man into the priesthood. This is easy enough to say, but this priest came to it after some anguish and struggle. He was open to the gift and was able to affirm it as one affirms an act of faith, for indeed the dynamic in the life of faith and in the acceptance of one's priestly vocation are basically the same. Both involve certitude and yet a certain obscurity or darkness as well.

Another example: I have known priests and seminarians who felt that the priesthood was something they wanted, but they did not sense it as a gift. They thought it came too much from themselves. While desiring the priesthood, they were quite unsure of whether God wanted it, and some were too paralyzed by fear to open up to God in order to see if it really was his desire. Yet all through the Scriptures, this dynamic of men and women coming before God to struggle with their vocation is common. How could it be less so for us? For priests, the experience of the apostles is normative. The bishop is a successor of the apostles, and the priest shares in the apostolic ministry and task: "Through the priesthood of the Bishop, the priesthood of the second order is incorporated in the apostolic structure of the Church . . . (cf. 2 Cor 5:20). This is the basis of the missionary character of every priest."[8]

We note that the twelve certainly received a personal call from God, yet their motivations needed to be transformed and changed:

> They came to Capernaum and, once inside the house, he began to ask them, "What were you arguing about on the way?" But they remained silent. They had been discussing among themselves on the way who was the greatest. Then he sat down, called the Twelve, and said to them, "If anyone wishes to be first, he shall be the last of all and the servant of all." (Mk 9:33-35)

To me the most interesting part of this passage relates to their silence: "They remained silent. They had been discussing among themselves on the way who was the greatest." They were ashamed to tell him what he already knew. Sound familiar? Such silence before Christ can prevent our grasp of the priesthood from coming to maturity. When we can share with Christ in prayer and in spiritual direction the weaknesses of our response and our fears, the work of grace is well begun. The passage from a rigidly idealistic priesthood to one that is real and gentle, one that needs divine help, has begun. The priest has begun to be a "man in relationship," as *Pastores Dabo Vobis* has it, because his relationships to bishops, brother priests, and the people he serves are now free, and are informed not by his own ego but by the life of the Holy Trinity. We have a chance now to see our priesthood more and more as a gift that is greater—oh, so much greater—than our weakness. There is room for grace now.

How else could Christ have reached us except through others? The very desire for the priesthood is itself a gift, but as with the apostles, it needs refinement and maturation. The priest is called to a higher and more complete sense of vocational acceptance. By this I do not mean that we are holier or wiser than those whom we serve. However, we are the ones who show them their vocation, by our preaching and by pastoral and spiritual counsel. So our sense of having been called must become ever clearer. How can we, with credibility, affirm and describe the vocation of our parishioners until we have recognized and accepted the authenticity of our own call?

Therefore, the priest must enter into a personal dynamic with Christ, as part of his daily life, in order to believe and accept this most consoling of truths, a truth that will mean even more to him as he enters the late afternoon and evening of his priesthood: "I have done with my life what God has wanted me to do." I do not believe there is any consolation for a priest greater than being able to say that with conviction and gratitude.

WANTED: BUT FOR WHAT?

The second question is related to the content of the call: Wanted for what? The priestly ministry is not made out of thin air. Christ has a work for the priest: the work of the Son of God. The very words that the priest repeats at the Eucharist and at Baptism are Christ's words. The absolution of sinners is done in his name and by the power of his redemption. The word that is preached is Christ's. Nothing the priest has in this ministry is his own. He preaches the word of another. He is sent by another. He is called to intimacy with another. The sacraments he confers, of which the Eucharist is the greatest, would not be anything except for the words of the other. Indeed, the sacraments are the actions of another. It is true that they are now the priest's words, but they are ultimately and first the words of Christ. They have no content except what he gives them. Thus we begin to see the true poverty of the priest.

This leads us to grasp another grace that Christ wishes to give. Slowly the priest is called to accept ever more deeply that the words of Christ must become his words: "This is my Body. This is my

Blood." The priest can never stay outside of these words; he must be offering himself with Christ while he says them. Slowly he realizes that his life is becoming a gift: "My sacrifice is like his. He offered himself—so must I. I will fail in it often, but I will keep returning to this offering." For the priest there is no other road to joy, and the earlier he grasps it, the more peace he will have and the more effective he will be. This internalization of the words and actions of Christ is presented to the priest in dramatic fashion on the day of his ordination, when the bishop presents to him the chalice and paten with these words: "Know what you are doing, and imitate the mystery you celebrate: model your life on the mystery of the Lord's cross."[9] *Pastores Dabo Vobis* expresses the same truth: "The priest is a living and transparent image of Christ the Priest."[10]

A QUESTION NOT ALWAYS FACED

When this communion is properly grasped, only then does the priest fully realize the basis for his relationship with his bishop, with other priests, and with the laity he serves. Fundamental to this understanding is the priest's conviction, as part of his maturing faith, that the call to be a priest has come from Jesus Christ. Like the apostles in Mark's Gospel, he has been called both to be with Christ and to be sent out by Christ (cf. Mk 3:13-14). But how hard it is for most to accept this call properly. Oftentimes it is accepted superficially—not truly considered, not fully embraced, and therefore not influential in one's life. Some do not examine it at all.

There are reasons for this, and they can be understood by examining the history of individuals called by God, in both the Old and New Testament. The reasons relate to fear, anxiety, and a sense of unworthiness. They are found in the responses of prophets and apostles: "I am too young"; "Woe is me"; "Depart from me, oh Lord, for I am a sinful man." Even Mary, though sinless, needed to hear the words: "Do not be afraid, Mary" (Lk 1:30). So did the apostles: "Do not be afraid; from now on you will be catching men" (Lk 5:10).

The fears are diverse: "The call may not be authentic. Look at my failure in life and in the ministry. I desire ministry, but does God desire it? Have I weighted too heavily the desires of others?" These fears must be overcome—and they can be overcome. In fact, I believe that the first and greatest grace that Jesus Christ wishes to give to each priest and to each candidate for the priesthood is the grace of believing and holding in his heart that the call has really come from Jesus Christ. This certainty can grow; and if it grows and the priest grasps it in faith, holds it, and says "yes" to it, he has found—or rather he has been given—and accepted the pearl of great price. No wonder Pope John Paul II makes clear that the intimacy between Christ and his priests arises as a result of the call that Christ has initiated.[11]

Acceptance of the grace of the vocational call and of the special communion with Jesus Christ that is part of the call—if that acceptance is authentic—does not bring the priest away from his people, but towards them. In fact, it leads him with a joyful heart to offer his life for them.

THE ROAD

Now it is necessary to shed some light on the continuing road towards a mature priestly life, a life that has set aside the false goals of ambition, popularity, and public recognition—a journey that only ends in heaven. How does one do this? How does a priest find his way on this road, so filled with thickets yet so promising for the joy and peace it will bring to him, and promising also for the Church?

First of all, it must be remembered that finding his way is a work of grace. The priest or the candidate for priesthood must be open to the grace of understanding his call more and more. If vocation to the priesthood is a gift, then the road to its full acceptance is also a gift. Like any work of grace, it requires our collaboration. It requires openness to the light that comes from God. This is not some mystical light given to the few. It is the grace that God hungers to give, and it is given amidst the priest's everyday life and, most of all, through his pastoral ministry and reflection. Surely this is what Pope John Paul II had in mind when he said to the priests of this country, "Priesthood is not merely a task which has been assigned. It is a vocation, a call to be heard again and again."[12]

For the priest then, acceptance requires openness. If, as Socrates said, "an unexamined life is not worth living," that is especially true for the priest. Because so much of his life consists in helping others to find their ways in life, he must have examined his own life with the help of the Holy Spirit.

THE PLACE OF SPIRITUAL DIRECTION

Spiritual direction often plays a central role in helping a priest to accept the call of Christ, and it must avoid two extremes. One is psychologism and the other is a kind of spiritualism. The first does not give sufficient place to the dynamic internal movement of grace; the second does not give due weight to the importance of emotions as part of human growth. Either approach leads to a priest who is not integrated. Grace works on our emotions and fears, bringing them to the surface, showing the road to maturity, and helping us to take it.

Christ had to clarify for the apostles some of the immaturity of their own priestly call in his response to James and John, who had watched their mother kneel before Christ to seek a special place:

> You know that the rulers of the Gentiles lord it over them, and the great ones make their authority over them felt. But it shall not be so among you. Rather, whoever wishes to be great among you shall be your servant; whoever wishes to be first among you shall be your slave. Just so, the Son of Man did not come to be served but to serve and to give his life as a ransom for many. (Mt 20:25-28)

So Christ will show a priest, and the priest or candidate for the priesthood will share with his director, these lesser motivations so they can be set aside and the call heard more clearly. I believe Christ is always trying to show us who we are, for such knowledge draws us into closer communion with him.

While there is not space here for a full analysis of the importance of spiritual direction, it is proper to note that spiritual direction, especially in the seminary, is both a science and an art. In these times, it is not valid, if indeed it ever was, to assign men who have had no training or experience, or who lack the capacity to discern a true vocation, to spiritual direction in the seminary. It is essential to the future of the Church that priests be trained in spiritual direction and give themselves to it full-time for a period of years, for part of their work is to be strong enough to urge those who are not called to the priesthood to step aside so they can find the place to which God is calling them. This takes a priest who has grown up spiritually and emotionally.

The priest is drawn to a more dynamic and yet more peaceful relationship with Christ, who is walking the road with him, when the priest faces, like the apostles, the lesser motivations of his response—always in the context of the infinite love of Christ, and with a spiritual director who understands this road, points out the light ahead, and encourages and welcomes a more mature acceptance of the call. The call is there for the priest. For most, it has always been there. Deep down they hope it to be so. But full acceptance of it takes time, prayer, spiritual direction, and a deeper sense of the love of Christ. It also takes another wonderful virtue: the courage to look at one's life. By the way, I remain convinced, from my experience in helping priests, that it is never too late to grasp these truths in a fresh way, never too late to say yes to Christ's call. While it is best if these matters can be faced—or at least begin to be faced—in the seminary, divine grace, understood properly (that is, dynamically), is always present, always inviting. It is never too late.

PRAYER

Much has been written in recent years about some of the beautiful methods of prayer, so distinctive in our spiritual tradition, such as *Lectio Divina* and the spiritual exercises of St. Ignatius. It may be, however, that not enough has been written and taught regarding conversation with God about our daily lives. Yet here is where both our vocation and our salvation are worked out. How can we say we have a close friendship with Jesus Christ if we do not share with him our deepest anxieties and worries, our hopes and desires, and if we do not share with him especially our desire to deepen and strengthen our acceptance and appreciation of this divine call? In this connection, I find consoling the well-known definition of prayer given by St. Theresa of Avila, another Doctor of the Church, in her autobiography: Prayer is conversation with someone who we know loves us.

One notices in *Pastores Dabo Vobis* a beautiful reflection on affective maturity. This also develops a root found in the documents of the Second Vatican Council. This maturity, so necessary for successful married life, as well as for the life of the consecrated celibate person, is not easily achieved. It is rarely achieved without true friendship, both with Christ and with other human beings. How beautiful is the priest as friend:

> Since the charism of celibacy, even when it is genuine and has proved itself, leaves [one's] affections and . . . instinctive impulses intact, candidates to the priesthood need an affective maturity which is prudent, able to renounce anything that is a threat to it, vigilant over both body and spirit, and capable of esteem and respect in interpersonal relationships between men and women.[13]

Such friendships are a gift from God and are usually his instruments in helping us to make a true gift of ourselves to others, a life to which the priest is obviously called. It can be quickly seen that these instruments—sound spiritual direction, friendships, and friendship with Christ through prayer—are all geared toward helping the priest come out of himself. They do not suppress his needs as a human being and a man; rather, they assist him in meeting these needs in a way that is orderly and is subject to his vocation and his priestly life. Many post-conciliar documents show how seriously the Church takes all this:

> The choice of priestly celibacy does not interfere with the normal development of a person's emotional life, but on the contrary it presupposes it.[14]

This [maturity] is all the more applicable when one is dealing with the formation of students in a seminary. This is
because God calls real men and if there are no real men,
there can be no call.[15]

Many years ago, I spent two weeks on Cape Cod. It was late spring,
before the visitors arrived. I was working on a course on the life of
faith, later to be presented to candidates for the priesthood. I remember it as a lovely time. Late each day after study, I would take a walk,
and this thought came to me—I am sure it was a grace—"Of all
these people that I am passing in shopping malls and along the
ocean, I am the only one committed to the priesthood and to a celibate way of life." I had a strong sense that it was the right place for
me, that even though I was the only priest among all these people, it
was right. I was in the place where I should be. It has always been
evident to me that this deepened sense, surely a gift, came during a
time when I had moved aside to pray and study. Of course, such a
conviction will be challenged as life goes on, but the challenges are
meant to strengthen the conviction.

Every day the priest meets and works with people whose lives,
while similar to his in Christian faith, are also quite different. They
are married and have children and grandchildren. The ones who
are not married are, for the most part, open to that vocation. The
priest knows that he too was open to marriage before becoming a
priest. Also, he does not see so many young men coming along to
dedicate themselves to the priesthood; nor does he see so many
consecrated religious, sisters and brothers, offering themselves to
God. These consecrated religious were often an inspiration to
priests in the past. In fact, it must be said that sisters teaching in

our schools were often the instrument that God used to draw many men to the priestly life.

On top of this, the misuse of sexuality in terms that many, including young people, find offensive has become part of our culture. The media proclaims, and one even hears it in the Church, that "sexual activity" must be part of the road to maturity. This is patently false. Commitment to a loving way of life, whether to celibate love or married love, requires true emotional maturity, and the intense currents that attack this today require an ever deeper, more mature commitment.

The Holy Father illustrated quite clearly the beautiful life that will result when fear is overcome and this journey is taken:

> The priest, who *welcomes* the call to ministry, is in a position to make this a loving choice, as a result of which the Church and souls become his first interest, and with this concrete spirituality he becomes capable of loving the universal Church and that part of it entrusted to him *with the deep love of a husband for his wife.*[16]

Priestly celibacy, like marriage, is a call to love. Priests who can love in this way are central to the new evangelization. Is this not what the Holy Father means when he says that the new evangelization must be new in method, in *ardor*, in expression?

This ardor, which relates to the expression of love, becomes disciplined and effective when the priest has accepted his priestly vocation and through the power of grace—grace helped by friendship—is able to achieve the capacity to make a gift of himself. Priests, like married people, are called to love.

The striking words of John Paul II in his first encyclical, repeated by him in *Pastores Dabo Vobis*, apply in a preeminent way to the priest: "Man cannot live without love. He remains a being that is incomprehensible for himself, his life is meaningless, if love is not revealed to him, if he does not encounter love, if he does not experience it and make it his own, if he does not participate intimately in it."[17]

THE GIFT

Christ's priesthood consisted of offering himself. So must the priest, for there is no priesthood but Christ's. The gift we offer is our very selves, our lives. This gift is renewed again and again each day through our ministry. We fail in it often, but we return to it always. The gift that the priest has received is nothing less than the divine love between Father and Son. The hours he spends in preparing a homily, his visits to the cancer ward, his conversations with young people, the time he spends hearing confessions, the training of catechists and other coworkers, his daily prayer, and his time of rest and recreation are the expressions of his love, making real his gift.

St. John Vianney, patron saint of parish priests, wrote the following: "The priest continues the work of redemption on earth. . . . If we really understood the priest on earth, we would die not of fright but of love. . . . The Priesthood is the love of the heart of Jesus."[18] This country pastor understood that the communion within the life of the Trinity was his to be lived and preached and made present in the Eucharist. He understood that it was a life of love. May the Holy Spirit open us to this love so that the whole Church will be richer through our lives and our work.

Taking this journey each day, we come to understand and joyfully accept what Pope John Paul II said to the priests of Ireland in the historic seminary at Maynooth in October 1979: "It is a great time to be a priest."

NOTES

1   John Paul II, *Pastores Dabo Vobis* (PDV) (*I Will Give You Shepherds*) (Washington, D.C.: United States Catholic Conference, 1992).

2   John Paul II, *Tertio Millennio Adveniente* (*On the Coming of the Third Millennium*) (Washington, D.C.: United States Catholic Conference, 1994), no. 18.

3   PDV, no. 16.

4   Ibid.

5   Ibid., no. 15.

6   Cf. Joseph Ratzinger, *Introduction to Christianity*, trans. J. R. Foster (New York: Seabury, 1969), p. 17.

7   Cf. John Paul II, first Holy Thursday Letter to Priests (1979), no. 5; John Paul II, Homily to Priests of the United States, Philadelphia (October 4, 1979), no. 1, in *Pilgrim of Peace* (Washington, D.C.: United States Catholic Conference, 1979).

8   PDV, no. 16.

9   Rite of Ordination of Deacons and Priests, no. 30.

10 PDV, no. 12.

11 Cf. John Paul II, Homily to the Priests of the United States, op. cit., no. 2.

12 Ibid., no. 1.

13 PDV, no. 44.

14 Sacred Congregation for Catholic Education, *Guide to Formation in Priestly Celibacy* (Washington, D.C.: United States Catholic Conference, 1974), no. 30.

15 Ibid., no. 19.

16 Cited in PDV, no. 23; emphasis added.

17 John Paul II, *Redemptor Hominis* (*Redeemer of Man*), no. 10; cited in PDV, no. 44.

18 Cited in *Catechism of the Catholic Church*, 2nd ed. (Washington, D.C.: United States Catholic Conference, 2000), no. 1589.

The Sacramental Identity of the Ministerial Priesthood:[1] "In Persona Christi"

Most Reverend Daniel M. Buechlein, OSB, STL
Archbishop of Indianapolis

Since Vatican Council II and the subsequent flourishing of the laity's collaboration in ministry, there has been a clarifying refinement of the Church's theological understanding of the identity of the ministerial priesthood. Various doctrinal statements of the Council set the stage: for example, *Lumen Gentium* and *Presbyterorum Ordinis*. Subsequent international synods of bishops and the writings of Pope John Paul II—particularly his apostolic letter *Pastores Dabo Vobis*— have provided a clear focus on priestly identity.

As we reflect on our identity as priests, we need to keep in mind that our identity is something more than the ministry we do. Yet these days we tend to understand and define the ministerial priesthood in terms of what we do—in terms of our pastoral activity, as distinguished from other ministries in the Church. There is a hazard in this. Important as our ministry is, definition on the basis of function alone, even sacramental ministry, doesn't really provide a satisfactory rationale for the distinctive identity of priests in the face of today's questions and concerns about priestly life and ministry.[2] And so it is important to reflect on the distinctive *nature* of the ministerial priesthood.

What is our Church's understanding of the priesthood as we cross the threshold of a new Christian millennium? The Second Vatican Council situated the ministerial priesthood within an ecclesial and pastoral perspective. While it revived the Church's understanding of the universal priesthood of Jesus, to whom all the baptized are configured, the Council also reasserted the Church's traditional doctrine that the priesthood of the ordained "differs essentially, and not only in degree" from the priesthood common to all the baptized.[3]

CHRIST AND THE CHURCH ARE SACRAMENTS

The proper context for understanding priestly identity is within the mystery of the Church. And of course, the starting point for understanding the mystery of the Church is the Incarnation of Jesus Christ, the Son of God. Our incarnational vision of Church is necessarily sacramental. And preeminently, the Eucharist maintains the Christ-centered nature of our Church's life as the Body of Christ. The Church is a body, a community; indeed, in the terms of the Second Vatican Council, we are a *communio*. The Church as a communion has been commissioned by Christ to provide a ministry of evangelization that is eschatological: that is, we are to proclaim the Gospel of Jesus Christ to the outer limits of the world and the outer limits of time. Our Church is ministerial and missionary in its fundamental orientation. And the Eucharist is the source and summit of all the Church is and does.

George H. Tavard summarizes this thought succinctly: "There is an identity in mystery between Church and Eucharist. The identity is between *Christ given for us,* the *Eucharist* in which we receive *Christ given for us,* the *ecclesia* into which we are built by *Christ given for us,* and the mission of the kingdom in which we expect and announce the return of *Christ given for us.*"[4]

Seen in this context, the identity of the ministerial priesthood is clearly and necessarily Christological and rooted in the Eucharist. Christ given for us is, after all, *the* Word and *the* gesture of eternal salvation who proceeds from God the Father. Christ is *the sacrament* of eternal salvation, and in these "last days," the Church is the primordial sacrament of Christ. The sacraments of the Church, instituted by Christ, provide the particular ways in which the Church is the primordial sacrament of eternal salvation—the way in which the Church is "the means" to salvation until the end of time. And central to everything, the source and summit of the Church's life, is the Eucharist, which is Christ given for us.

THE MYSTERY OF THE PRIESTHOOD IS ROOTED IN THE MYSTERY OF THE CHURCH[5]

Within a theology that explicitly considers the Church as the sacrament of the risen Body of Jesus Christ, the High Priest, it is possible to understand more fully who we are as priests. God chose a particular moment and place in the human world, and he sent his Son to bring grace and mercy in human word and in human gesture. This *is* sacrament. Christ is *the* sacrament; he is *the* visible Word and gesture. He *is* the Father's prodigious mercy made flesh—salvation made visible in our history.

The words and gestures of Jesus were not mere "play-acting" nor were they a dated message *about* salvation. The word and action of Jesus were at one and the same time a sign of grace and timeless grace itself; they were and are eternal salvation in visible form. Not just a message about salvation, Jesus is the effective sacrament of our salvation forever.

CHRIST IS *THE* HIGH PRIEST

The letter to the Hebrews celebrates Christ the High Priest. No one except Jesus has, by right and in fact, entered God's own sanctuary, the place of radical nearness to and intimacy with God. Nor has anyone except Jesus been once and for all immolated as the sacrifice that totally belongs to God. No one except Jesus has entered the heavenly sanctuary to present his own blood in an unrepeatable sacrifice that totally returns to God what is God's. In Christ, perfect victim and perfect minister of the altar are joined in the fullness of priesthood. In the very act of going to the Father with his whole life, Jesus is "consecrated" and set apart as *the high priest*. In all truth, Christ is the only priest. This consecration of Christ in the unique fullness of priesthood was achieved in the awesome mystery of his death, resurrection, and ascension.

But what about now? Jesus is no longer visible to us in his human body. Surely the salvation intended for us should be humanly available to us even after Jesus the Christ returned to the sanctuary of the Father as eternal High Priest. Jesus, the sacrament of salvation, must be available to us in some form that we can see and experience as human persons "in these last days."

THE CHURCH IS THE SACRAMENT OF CHRIST
CALLING ALL TO UNITY

The Church declares explicitly that she is the sacrament of Christ. "In these last days," the Church is the active presence of Christ in time and place, visible to all. The very meaning of the Church is caught up in the activity of God calling a people to himself in space and time through his Son. (It is the continuation of salvation history in "the last days.") It was the mission of Jesus to draw people to union with him (and with each other) in his Mystical Body. As High Priest and Head of the Body, Jesus continues to exercise his pastoral leadership in the Church today. Indeed, because he is the Bridegroom of the Church, his call to union with himself and the Father by the power of the Holy Spirit is the call to salvation. Salvific communion is the very purpose of the perfect sacrifice that he offered on the altar of the cross and presents to his Father in the heavenly sanctuary. As Head of the Body and High Priest and Bridegroom, Jesus calls all members to communion. The Church is the visible sign and the reality of this *unifying* activity of Christ.

THE CHURCH IS CHRIST'S BODY CALLED INTO UNITY

The Church is also the visible sign and the reality of the Christian community's activity of *being united* in Christ. The Church is both the sacrament of Jesus calling *and* the sacrament of his Body being called to unity. Somehow in mystery the Church must be both Head and mystical Body, both mystical Bridegroom and Bride.

The fathers of the Second Vatican Council, drawing on the images used by Paul in his letter to the Colossians (Col 1:15-18), describe the "corporate Christ" like this: "The head of this body is Christ. He is the image of the invisible God and in him all things came into being. He is before all creatures and in him all things hold together. He is the head of the body which is the Church."[6]

But if the whole Christ is both Head and members, then the sacrament of the risen Christ must visibly be both Head and members. If the risen Christ is Head and members, the sacrament of the risen Christ in turn must visibly be both Head and members. If he is High Priest, he must visibly be so now.

PRIESTS: CONFIGURED TO THE PERSON OF CHRIST, HEAD OF THE BODY

The Second Vatican Council states that those who receive the sacrament of Holy Orders represent Christ as Head of the Church and as High Priest. *Sacrosanctum Concilium* (*Constitution on the Sacred Liturgy*) says the priest at the Eucharist, which embodies the very mystery of Christ among us, is to be one "who, in the person of Christ, presides over the assembly."[7] *Presbyterorum Ordinis* (*Decree on Priestly Life and Ministry*) reads, "The priesthood of priests . . . is nevertheless conferred by its own particular sacrament. Through that sacrament, priests by the anointing of the Holy Spirit are signed with a special character and so are configured to Christ the priest in such a way that they are able to act in the person of Christ the head."[8]

The ministerial priesthood is the visible presence of Christ as he calls all people to unity. The ministerial priesthood is a sacrament for the unity of the Church, a sacrament of Christ the pastor and the Bridegroom. The ministerial priesthood is the visible presence of Christ the High Priest in the Church in "the last days." It is, therefore, the sacrament of Christ as Head of the Body, High Priest, and Bridegroom.

Who are priests? We are living "sacraments." To use another image, we are icons of the pastoral leadership of the One who calls the People of God to unity, and we are the icon of the priesthood of Jesus.[9] What are priests? We are the sacrament of Jesus the pastor and priest "in the last days."

Priests: Called by Christ Through the Bishop to a "Communitarian Form"

The power to be a sacrament of the unifying leadership of Christ and of his unique priestly role is conferred in ordination. It is important to recall at this point that "Christ himself, in his Spirit, calls a man to represent him as Shepherd" (and High Priest and Bridegroom); "the call comes not from the body of the Church, but from Christ as mediated through the bishop."[10] Ordination is not an empowerment by the body of the Church to act on its behalf; rather, it is an empowerment of the priest by God to act in the person of Christ the High Priest for and with the Church. As that empowerment is mediated through the bishop, a bond of communion with the bishop—and with the collegium of other priests called by Christ through the bishop—marks an important characteristic of our unique identity as priests. In *Pastores Dabo Vobis*, the Holy Father wrote, "By its very nature, the ordained ministry can be carried out only to the extent that the priest is united to Christ through sacramental participation in the priestly order, and thus to the extent that he is in hierarchical communion with his own Bishop. The ordained ministry has a radical '*communitarian form*' and can only be carried out as a 'collective work.'"[11] Our identity precludes a sense of being independent agents in ministry. We are a priestly collegium that serves in communion with our bishop.

Ontological Transformation by Ordination

As the Council taught, by the anointing of the Holy Spirit in the sacrament of Holy Orders we are configured to Christ in such a unique manner that we are empowered to act in the person of Christ the Head of the Body, the High Priest, and Bridegroom. Pope John Paul II has written that by virtue of this consecration, the priest participates ontologically in the priesthood of Christ and "becomes a man of the sacred."[12]

The Holy Father has also stated, "Just as in the Mass the Holy Spirit brings about the transubstantiation of the bread and wine into the Body and Blood of Christ, so also in the sacrament of holy orders he effects the priestly or episcopal consecration."[13]

By the power of the Holy Spirit, at our consecration in ordination, we are so configured to Christ the Priest that our very being is transformed: "The priest then is not a 'substitute' or a stand-in for Christ like a proxy at a meeting. Or a substitute teacher in a grade school. The priest makes Christ the Shepherd present in a way similar to the way in which the Eucharistic Bread is not just a 'sign' that Christ is present but rather the sacrament of the Eucharist makes Him present in a special way."[14] The ordinand *is* priest in the person of Christ the High Priest. We are not substitutes. The ministerial priest *does not merely do* priestly things. We are ontologically "men of the sacred," as our Holy Father says.

MINISTRY FLOWS FROM SACRAMENTAL IDENTITY

By virtue of this sacramental consecration, we priests have the power to preside in the person of Christ at the Eucharist. And let us note here that as the Eucharist is constitutive of the existence of the Church, so is the priesthood constitutive for the life of the Church. The person of Christ acts through us. By virtue of consecration in Orders we have the power to absolve sins and to be the instrument of paschal reconciliation in the person of Christ the High Priest. In our role as "sacrament" of Jesus the Shepherd and the Bridegroom, we are authorized by God himself through the mediation of the Church to proclaim the Lord's call to unity; and we are authorized to draw together all those who, by their

Baptism, exercise another form of priesthood: membership in the Body called to worship the Father in spirit and in truth. Because of our unique ontological relationship to Christ the High Priest and Head of the Church by priestly consecration, our ministry is unlike any other ministry in the Church.

PRIESTS: MOST VISIBLY SACRAMENTS OF CHRIST THE HIGH PRIEST AT THE "TABLE OF THE LORD"

Just as the entire community is most visibly the Body of Christ—that is, most visibly Church—when it is gathered around the table of the Lord both to hear the Lord's word and to be fed by his Body (and thus to worship the Father in spirit and in truth), so we are most visibly the sacrament of Christ the Head and Christ the Priest when we preside at the Eucharist. We priests are most visibly who we are in the community at the table of the Lord—at "the breaking of the Bread."

In relationship to the faithful who rightfully claim their part in the worship and unifying service of the Church, at the Eucharist we priests are to be leaders and signs of the unifying activity of Jesus. To claim such leadership takes the understanding, courage, and humility to be no more (and no less) than authentically designated leaders who serve in the manner of him who came to serve.

PRIESTS: ICONS OF CHRIST THE SHEPHERD, PRIEST, BRIDEGROOM

Dominican scholar J. M. R. Tillard uses the Eastern understanding of "icon" to explain who priests are. We recall that icons are not ordinary paintings; they are images that somehow contain the very mystery they represent, and thus they draw those who gaze on them into mystery. We priests are icons of Jesus, as the one who serves unity, as the one and only High Priest. We are also icons of Jesus as the Bridegroom of the Church.

There are other icons of Jesus. Can we not say that the poor, the suffering, and the oppressed are icons of Jesus, the sacrificial victim? Can we not see the face of Jesus in every sister and brother, all of whom together are to be icons of the holiness of Jesus, who leads us to worship "in spirit and in truth"?

Yet it is distinctive and essentially different to be the icon of Jesus as one who calls to unity through the exercise of pastoral leadership and an icon of Jesus as High Priest, the one who offers his very own blood that has saved us all. It is distinctive to be an icon of Jesus the Bridegroom of the Church. In these days of politicization it is important to remember that this distinction is to serve communion in the Church, not division.

We should note another characteristic of our priestly identity that flows from Christ as Bridegroom. In *Pastores Dabo Vobis,* Pope John Paul II writes, "The Church, as the Spouse of Jesus Christ, wishes to be loved by the priest in the total and exclusive manner in which Jesus Christ her Head and Spouse loved her. Priestly celibacy, then, is the gift of self *in* and *with* Christ *to* his Church and expresses the priest's service to the Church in and with the Lord."[15] In the Western tradition we priests live in identity with the celibate pastoral love of Christ the Bridegroom of the Church.

PRIESTS: ANOINTED BY THE HOLY SPIRIT TO BE SERVANTS

By anointing and consecration at Baptism, by the power of the Holy Spirit, all the initiated are joined to Christ in worship of the Father and in service of Christ's Body. All Christians are initiated, if you will, into the common priesthood of a holy life. The baptized are marked for life with an "indelible character or seal." Like all the baptized, we priests are once and for all claimed for Christ and are configured to Christ.

At ordination, we priests are further consecrated by the Holy Spirit with an indelible character as we are configured to Christ the Head of the Body of the Church and High Priest. As ministerial priests, we participate in the High Priesthood of Jesus and are the *means* or the *channel* by which the universal priesthood of the holy life can be realized in the Church. As ordained priests, we are called to serve the bond between Christ the High Priest and the community of believers who belong to the universal priesthood. We are not only icons of Jesus the Priest and Shepherd, we are also the *Douloi*, servants of the one priesthood.[16] If you will, servanthood is central to our identity as priests.

Just as we are able to participate in the priesthood of a holy life through the gift of the Spirit received in baptismal consecration, so it is by the gift of the same Spirit received in the consecration of Holy Orders that we are able to be at the service of the priesthood of Jesus. By ordination, we are empowered to serve the priesthood of Jesus by sharing the very same Spirit in whom Jesus accomplished his priestly ministry.

Far from being mere "mechanical instruments," far from being mere "blurred photographs" of Jesus as High Priest and Head of the Body, "the Spirit wills to draw us into a communion of *behavior* with the One we serve."[17] The icon metaphor works particularly well here. There is a difference between a photograph and an icon, in the sense that in an icon there is more than simply the pictorial presence.

Tillard says so aptly: "At ordination the Spirit wants to unite us as closely as possible with what lay at the heart of the priesthood of Jesus: His gift of all of Himself for those who belonged to Him."[18] The self-emptying gift of his very self, and his death, are nothing but the manifestation of who Jesus is at the deepest level of his being, as the one who comes from God and goes to God.

As Priests Our Very Life Is Consecrated for Service

Consecration to serve the priesthood of Jesus, therefore, is to serve with one's very life, not just by some functions or tasks. Participation in the priesthood of Jesus by the grace of Holy Orders must be understood as communion in the Spirit with the priesthood of Jesus. Hence personal communion with the self-emptying Jesus is part of the charism of Orders. Configuration to Christ the Priest and Shepherd and generous service to his Body go together.

Communion in the Spirit with the Self-Emptying Christ Is Key to Understanding Our Identity as Priests

Herein lies a key to understanding the permanence of our commitment in the ministerial priesthood, the ontological nature of our priestly relationship to Jesus the Priest, and the call to live our entire priestly life in the simple way in which Jesus lived.

Communion in the Spirit with Jesus is effected by sacramental anointing and consecration. Accepting the call to ministerial priesthood is more than accepting a different "lifestyle." Unless one's life is to be a mere lifeless echo of what others say about the word of God and a lifeless drama of sacramental ministry, our own experience of communion with Jesus and priestly service in ministry are joined. Our challenge is to know Christ as the center of our ministry and to keep him there.

We are called to be icons of Christ in the most dynamic sense. And surely, authenticity means personal communion with the mystery of Jesus. And so we become humbly aware that if our identity with Christ is to be as humanly authentic as possible, personal intimacy with him is crucial. We need that special bond of intimacy that is anchored in the Eucharist and nourished before the tabernacles in our churches and chapels. Our priestly identity is anchored and nurtured in the Eucharist, which impels us to self-emptying service in ministry.

CHRIST ACTS THROUGH THE HUMANITY OF PRIESTS FOR THE GOOD OF THE CHURCH

One of the profound implications of the mystery of the ministerial priesthood conferred by ordination is the doctrine that the person of Christ the High Priest, through his Holy Spirit, acts through us priests for the good of the Church, even when we are personally unworthy. As the *Catechism of the Catholic Church* teaches, "As fire transforms into itself everything it touches, so the Holy Spirit transforms into the divine life whatever is subjected to his power."[19] By ordination, we priests are sealed by the Holy Spirit with an indelible character by which we are so configured to Christ that when acting in the sacramental forum, even if we are personally unworthy, the sacrament is nonetheless conferred. We speak of the sacramental doctrine, *ex opere operato*.

Yet if and when we priests are not trying to be who we say we are and who we appear to be, then the People of God do not have a truly authentic image or icon of Christ the Priest and Pastor. If and when our own vision of priestly life and ministry is blurred, then the Body of Jesus is truly wounded.

And what if we are such priests? Being a "lifeless echo" is a miserable kind of emptiness, not the life-giving, self-emptying love of Jesus. Therefore, it is so important that the very depth of our lives as priests be confronted totally and daily by our unique relationship to Jesus the High Priest—and at the source and summit of all life, namely the Eucharist. We understand that prayer before the Blessed Sacrament is the premier way in which we extend our consciousness of the eucharistic mystery beyond the altar of sacrifice.

CONSECRATION BY THE SPIRIT MAKES AN EXISTENTIAL CLAIM ON PRIESTS

The priesthood as sacrament of Jesus the Shepherd, High Priest, and Bridegroom makes *an existential claim* on our very person as priests. True, the effectiveness of the sacramental ministry being done in the person of Jesus—the objective "power" of grace—is there no matter what quality of ministry is given. Still, must not our disposition mirror the self-emptying leadership and the priestly act of Jesus? Unquestionably, how we serve the priesthood of Jesus affects the faith of the Christian community. Hence, our priestly ministry is not merely a career or part-time profession. It is a great deal more than living a "style" of life. To speak of priesthood as a lifestyle is to subvert the true depth of priestly identity. Our very lives as priests are the instrument of the priestly ministry of Jesus.

Let me simply say that our identity as icons of Jesus—pastor and priest—allows for the elaboration of other facets of priestly identity in ministry that are present by implication. Certainly we priests are configured to Jesus the Teacher and Prophet, which is implicit in his Headship of the Body. Every other aspect of our ministry as priests flows from our sacramental configuration to Jesus the Head of the Body. Our very life exists *in persona Christi Capitis*. This awesome mystery can only move us priests to humble, fervent, and grateful prayer before the Tabernacle of him whose priesthood we serve. Daily we are moved to a double act of faith: (1) We believe that Christ calls us to this awesome ministry of his; and (2) since he does so, he gives us the grace we need to live this awesome call in humble service. Our challenge is to keep Christ as the center of our hearts and minds!

NOTES

1   This essay is taken from a series of lectures given as part of a course on priestly ministry and spirituality at Saint Meinrad Seminary, Ind., in 1986.

2   Cf. Mark O'Keefe, *In Persona Christi: Reflections on Priestly Identity and Holiness* (St. Meinrad, Ind.: Abbey Press, 1998).

3   Cf. Second Vatican Council, *Lumen Gentium* (LG) (*Dogmatic Constitution on the Church*), no. 10. In Austin Flannery, ed., *Vatican Council II: The Conciliar and Post Conciliar Documents*, new rev. ed. (Northport, N.Y.: Costello Publishing Company, 1996).

4   George H. Tavard, *A Theology for Ministry*, vol. 6, *Theology and Life Series* (Wilmington, Del.: M. Glazier, 1983), p. 54.

5   Much of the theme of this chapter is based upon a wonderful little study by Jean M. R. Tillard, "The Ordained 'Ministry' and the 'Priesthood' of Christ," *One in Christ* 14 (1978): 231-246. The article first appeared in *Irenikon* no. 2 (1976): 147-166.

6   LG, no. 7.

7　Second Vatican Council, *Sacrosanctum Concilium* (*Constitution on the Sacred Liturgy*), no. 33. In Flannery, op. cit.

8　Second Vatican Council, *Presbyterorum Ordinis* (*Decree on the Ministry and Life of Priests*), no. 2. In Flannery, op. cit.

9　The image of "icon" is used by J. M. R. Tillard, op. cit., p. 240.

10　O'Keefe, op. cit., p. 17.

11　John Paul II, *Pastores Dabo Vobis* (PDV) (*I Will Give You Shepherds*) (Washington, D.C.: United States Catholic Conference, 1992), no. 17.

12　John Paul II, *The Church: Mystery, Sacrament, Community: A Catechesis on the Creed*, vol. 4 (Boston: Pauline Books and Media, 1998), p. 304.

13　John Paul II, *Gift and Mystery: On the Fiftieth Anniversary of My Priestly Ordination* (New York: Doubleday, 1996), p. 44.

14　O'Keefe, op. cit., p. 18.

15　PDV, no. 29.

16　Cf. Tillard, op. cit., p. 238.

17　Ibid.

18　Ibid.

19　*Catechism of the Catholic Church*, 2nd ed. (Washington, D.C.: United States Catholic Conference, 2000), no. 1127.

COLLABORATORS IN MINISTRY: THE BISHOP AND HIS PRIESTS

Most Reverend Robert N. Lynch
Bishop of St. Petersburg

Several years ago, while serving my last year as general secretary of the episcopal conference of the United States (NCCB), I was in Rome during *Ferro Augusto*, those final two weeks in the summer when almost every Italian leaves the cities and heads for either the beach or the mountains. Many restaurants are closed, and only visitors like myself and a few others who cannot leave the city remain. I remember one Sunday evening when I joined two friends who are priests for dinner in Rome at a lovely outdoor restaurant on Montemario, overlooking the city. At some point during the meal, one of my priest friends asked what I suspect was a rhetorical question: "Are there any bishops in the States who are universally genuinely loved by their priests?"

I rose to the bait and suggested a friend of mine who was an archbishop in a very large diocese. Then I somewhat negated my nomination by suggesting that undoubtedly some in his archdiocese did not appreciate his gifts and were probably not so well disposed toward him, although I also opined that his support had grown stronger throughout his years as ordinary.

The second priest said that he was certain that the particular bishop I had nominated would not pass the test. Listening to him, I suggested that perhaps his own archbishop might meet the test proposed in our friend's question. I recounted how at a recent meeting with his priests, that same archbishop was surprised when one of the senior priests in the archdiocese rose and said something to the effect that "throughout his life he had prayed for a courageous leader in the office of bishop and that God had answered his prayers with the example of the incumbent." The intervention was followed by long and sustained applause by the entire presbyterate, lasting almost seven minutes, I was told. "Yes, indeed," replied the other priest at the table. "There is no doubt in my mind that my archbishop does indeed enjoy the respect and support of the overwhelming majority of his priests."

I recalled that dinner as I was thinking about this essay, which deals with the relationship between a bishop and his priests. Since I know the aforementioned individual reasonably well, I thought I might use him as a paradigm for this essay and offer some reflections—admittedly not borne of long experience as a residential bishop, but at least springing from some of the things that I have learned in my soon-to-be completed four years as ordinary.

This archbishop, who seemed to enjoy the support of his priests, would probably be pleased to have the following descriptions applied to him: courageous, collegial, compassionate, creative, and very much of-the-Church—even though some might perceive him as "pushing the envelope" from time to time. I will expand on each of these *c* words slightly and then reflect on the failures and limited success of my own ministry in meeting the very high standard of this particular chap.

I think our priests want us to be collegial in the years ahead. They have as much and sometimes more of a stake in the decisions that we make for our dioceses than many of us bishops. Oftentimes they have to live with the consequences of our decisions long after we are retired, dead, or transferred. The only way to begin to break down the attitude of "us vs. the chancery" is to bring the priests into the thought, planning, and decision-making processes that will ultimately affect the lives of many.

If I may express my own personal feeling, I respect and enjoy the five-times-a-year meetings of our diocesan priests' council. These priests have been of enormous help to me in setting the direction for my pastoral ministry. They have not always agreed with me in the issues that I have placed before them; but on those occasions, their wisdom and counsel proved more correct than my own early read. When they have disagreed, they have always done so with an appreciation that the decisions were rightfully mine, but I would have been foolish to disregard their input and counsel.

With the single exception of awarding papal honors to priests and laity, I have consulted them on everything. Utilizing input received from the deaneries, the priest councillors have brought back to the table the feeling of the "fathers" on issues of consequence to them. For example, I wanted to introduce RENEW 2000 in our diocese but knew I should not do so until the priests decided that it would be a good thing for their parishes and themselves. For another example, I wanted to begin a lay pastoral ministry institute to train lay people and certify them for work in the Church but knew it would not work unless the priests saw a benefit in it. In both cases, we made use of the deanery meetings and several discussions at the priests' council before moving ahead. I have not mandated either program in the parishes, but RENEW is underway in fifty-seven of seventy-two parishes (several had already begun other programs of renewal such as FOLLOW ME! and Christ Renews His Parish, which has been around for quite a while). Almost 95 percent of the parishes have sent people to the lay pastoral ministry institute. I hope this high level of acceptance is due in part to a collegial approach.

I am now somewhat worried that in the past four years we have tried too much and that I have taxed the parish priests too greatly. Of course, I will ask the priests what they themselves think.

The only thing lost to a bishop who chooses a strong collegial approach to his relationship with his priests is the final trace of autocracy in the Church. The late Joseph Cardinal Bernardin was often kidded for his unfailing dedication to consultation. When the cardinal was falsely accused of sexual misconduct, one of his brother bishops—in a moment of dark humor in an otherwise bleak time—suggested that the accusation could not be true: "Joe, you would have consulted with at least six people and one consultative body before agreeing to anything like that." It was one of the few humorous moments in an otherwise tragic time, but the cardinal was pleased that his reputation for collegial sharing was still intact.

Our priests want us to share with them our dreams and visions, to consult with them on things that will ultimately affect their lives and to affirm their vision of where the Church might be headed and how best we might get there.

Courage is slightly more elusive but just as important in the relationship that a bishop has with his priests. I think our priests are, by and large, courageous men in and of themselves. It takes courage to present oneself week after week to a parish or school community and proclaim the Gospel of Jesus Christ, in and out of season. They are often called upon to make tough calls in the lives of their parishioners, and they often exhibit high levels of personal courage as well.

No priest has asked me in these past four years to take a position other than that clearly articulated and taught by the Church, but most look to me to display some courage in facing the real problems the Church is encountering today. They want their bishop to speak out against injustice toward migrants, the marginalized, the outcasts of society, and sometimes even those who feel they are on the fringe of the Church. They want me, or so it would seem, to speak honestly about human failure in the priesthood—but also to speak with equal or more forceful courage in pointing out the good that priests, deacons, religious, and laity do, not only in the Church but also in society.

I perceive they also wish me to be courageous in facing a somewhat uncertain future. Like many dioceses, my own is not currently replete with vocations to the priesthood and religious life. We are working on it, but any success we ultimately have will be years in coming to tangible fruition. I sense that the priests of my diocese don't want me to conduct business as usual but to show some courage in proposing strategies that will work for the Church until the decline of clergy can be reversed.

I also think the priests want to see courage in their bishop in carrying out the decisions and programs that have been collegially arrived at. It is one thing to drive decisions; it is yet another to personally lead in carrying them out. The best things that we have done in our diocese are the things we have done together. We are committed in the spring of 2000 to a diocese-wide effort to renew the sacrament of Reconciliation. To lift this up in the minds of the faithful, the priests and I have decided to spend thirteen nights together in thirteen parishes of the diocese to conduct communal penance services that will use the second rite. I will preside and preach at all thirteen (over three weeks), and the priests have promised that they will be present to hear individual confessions and to absolve sins. At this writing, I cannot predict how it will ultimately turn out, but I think if it has any chance of succeeding, I needed to show by my presence that this is as important to me as it is to the priests.

Most of the older and middle-aged priests have concerns about women in society and the Church. They would like to see me lead in courageously offering to competent women every opportunity that does not require ordination. Priests tend to be "inclusive" in their view of the Church and don't desire to exclude people from the life of the Church. Again, none have ever asked me, and I doubt if they will go against clear church teaching; but many have asked me to do what I can to make our local church more welcoming, hospitable, and open—a sanctuary for those who fear for their lives, and safe harbor for those who find life burdensome and troubling.

Compassion in a bishop seems like an automatic "slam dunk," but it is not always easy. In today's Church, the bishop is often at the vortex of strong feelings from every segment of church life. Even in relationships with his priests, the bishop can often feel like he is on the "hot seat." Some may wish he were more traditional, while others would like him to move faster, begin new changes, and lead more assertively. Every bishop, when he is ordained, feels that the priests especially have great expectations of him—perhaps even unrealistic expectations.

I have found the fragility of the diocesan priesthood to be much more of a challenge than I ever imagined prior to becoming a bishop. While at the NCCB, I would hear stories about challenges that bishops faced in their dioceses, but I think I was ill prepared for what I actually found. It is in reaching to those among the presbyterate who are hurting (or perceived as hurting) that the bishop has his greatest opportunity to exercise the charism of compassion.

Every bishop knows the heartache of compassionately listening while one of his brothers informs him of a decision to leave ministry and pursue marriage. Many bishops know the challenge to compassion occasioned by that first conversation with a priest accused of sexual misconduct. To listen compassionately while still making decisions for the good of both the Church and the priest is an incredible challenge and requires every interpersonal gift that the bishop can command.

I have not always done that well in the first four years of my ministry as bishop. It is hard not to be defensive sometimes. It is hard not to be overly judgmental sometimes. It is hard not to leap to conclusions, sometimes before the priest has even stated his case. Yet somehow every bishop has to protect his opportunity to apply compassion to the deepest concerns and pains of his priests.

The bishop needs his priests to help each other. I am convinced that when it comes to priests with problems, I am something akin to what the Navy used to call the "damage control officer." In the Navy, and in diocesan life, the damage control officer is called only after the conflagration (inner or outer) has broken out, and the only thing he can do is try to arrest it from spreading. Others have to help fight the fire.

I also learned rather quickly that I am not capable of solving every problem that arises with individual members of my presbyterate. Some need time for healing, and others need to see a specialist other than the bishop. But I have to listen with concern and compassion. Priests also need to understand that concern and compassion can be present even when they do not get the answer they have sought in coming to the bishop. Saying "no" can sometimes be a loving act. The bishop sometimes has to precipitate a crisis just to get someone's attention. None of us like to do that, but there are many cases when intervention is necessary.

One of my priests, on his return from a residential treatment facility for alcohol-related problems, told me about how lovingly the bishops were spoken of by men in recovery but how disliked were the bishops' representatives for the interventions. Those in recovery called these men "liquor vicars"; their stock was not high. The conventional wisdom might be that the bishop should preserve his right to intervene later in the process, but for the moment I still think that the bishop, at least in a small- or medium-sized diocese, has to apply the exercise of "tough love" personally and with firmness and compassion.

Admittedly, this is one of the most difficult aspects of the bishop's relationship with his priests, and others certainly approach it differently; but I have been asked to reflect on where I am in my ministry of bishop, and I believe that while the exercise of authority is sometimes absolutely necessary, the application of compassionate listening and direction also helps.

Unlike St. Paul, it is hard for most of us to be all things to all people. But if someone says of me at the end of my time that I was a compassionate listener, I will gladly accept that accolade.

Nothing helps a bishop in his relationship with his priests as much as the application of creativity. The brothers get tired of repetition and sameness. They respond well when things are slightly different from the year before or when something is offered that is truly unique and different.

Chrism Masses and whatever precedes and follows them are moments when a certain creativity can be applied. The annual convocations are another time when something can be different from the year before. In our diocese, we decided to stop calling the convocation "the annual retreat" and allow it to be both a time for prayer and a time for continuing education. We have had wonderful presenters (about three or four each year) and great discussions arising from them; three years ago we introduced a bishop (someone other than myself) to serve as a spiritual moderator for the three full days together (he preaches at the liturgy of the hours and at Mass). That bishop gets to do what I seldom have an opportunity to do: to prove that we in the episcopacy do understand the intricacies of the spiritual life of priests. It was a small but creative change in how we do things and has been well received.

Most pastors carry a heavy burden of finance on their shoulders. There are two ways of approaching this, or so it would seem to me. The first is to say, "Yes, that is precisely what being a pastor requires"; but the second is to find ways of easing the burden without putting the patrimony and treasure of God's people at risk. Creativity does wonders here for the morale of those priests who think they will never get out of debt or who bear scars and anger for decisions made by those who preceded them.

Creatively addressing the *ethos* of the chancery or pastoral center to make it more responsive to the needs of the priests and pastors is also a challenge that can bear great fruit for the relationship between pastors and their bishop. In too many cases, priests have the perception that the chancery thinks of them as local branch managers who need a signal from the home office for every major initiative, instead of thinking of the home office as being at the service of the pastors and priests.

With a few exceptions, time and again every study has revealed overwhelming support among the bishops for their national episcopal conference. Ideologically some may not agree with the actions of the Liturgy Committee or the Doctrine Committee or the Communications Committee or the Marriage and Family Life Committee (all randomly chosen here), but most bishops will say that the conference staff envisions themselves as being at the service of all. That kind of perception is something that many bishops are trying to bring to their own diocesan efforts; and when the perception is creatively applied, it is fun to watch the results. The largest and smallest parishes receive the same level of attention, and no question is so far off the mark as not to deserve an answer.

Creating a climate of trust oftentimes demands a level of creativity. The other *c*'s that I have detailed above have a lot to do with creating a climate of trust; sometimes there is little a bishop can do in his relationship with his priests because, for whatever reason, trust does not seem possible. Even though most of us try to act fraternally with our brothers in the presbyterate, sometimes the priest himself will just not move beyond suspicion or caution. I have found that many situations involving relationships between priests and bishops arise from the priest's own family life, which fashions his view of authority. The priest's relationship with his father often determines and guides the relationship between the priest and his bishop. If anger, resentment, or distrust of lawful and legitimate authority is present, then many times this will transfer into the priest's life in the Church. Breaking down these historical barriers requires a certain amount of creativity on the part of the bishop.

I believe that I may be a source of disappointment to some among my youngest clergy. Their hopes and aspirations for the Church differ markedly from my own. It is too facile to say that younger priests today long for the Church prior to the Second Vatican Council. It is also too facile to try to label the younger clergy with an ideological tag. Their hopes are much more rooted in a return to authority and in, perhaps, a clearer articulation of right and wrong than I seem willing to make. On the other hand, I know that 80 percent of my clergy do not wish to see a return to an authoritarian model. In fact, most priests are happy to be left alone in their ministry, with little or no moments of contact with the bishop.

I have made an effort in each of my first four years to create an environment whereby the priests collectively and individually may speak to me without fear or favor. I have invited them all to my home to break bread and to discuss common issues of concern. While I have practically killed my housekeeper in the process, the relaxed environment of home and board has allowed for a zesty discussion of issues of concern. I think it incumbent upon bishops to search creatively for ways in which the priests can speak their minds to one another and to their bishop without worrying about the consequences. The office seldom provides the right environment, for it contains every sign antithetical to openness and dialogue: a carpet to be called upon, people watching who comes and goes, and a strict schedule of appointments that suggests that every human problem can be resolved in thirty- or sixty-minute increments.

Today I believe a bishop must be very open to the application of the psychological sciences in the lives of his priests. Therapeutic counseling is here to stay and is a necessity for many of our employees, priests included (maybe even bishops, at times). Leadership in the Church must constantly search for creative ways in which to engage the psychological sciences and place them at the service of our co-workers. It is a part of the "damage control" of which I spoke earlier.

Finally, I am brought to the need for the bishop to be a man of the Church. Something so patently obvious is much more difficult in today's world to grasp and embrace. "Church" has so many definitions: local (diocesan or parochial), universal (the role of the papacy and the curia), national (the episcopal conference), and provincial (state episcopal conferences and regional groupings). I think it safe to say that if one were to ask most priests which of the definitions above he wished his bishop to concentrate on, it would be "local." But that is not so easy.

Furthermore, most of us would say that the chances of our ministry being enriched by our engagement with the larger Church is also true. Each has a chance of supporting the other. Perhaps an example would be in order. My priests have felt for a long time that here in the state of Florida especially, the assault on human life represented by our state's electric chair cried out for prophetic addressing. Most of them knew that this was not a popular cause to espouse and that many Catholics would not agree with them. Florida began executing again about a decade or more ago and currently has about 350 people on death row, awaiting an electric chair that seems cruel and unusual to many. But it was lonely in the public square until in 1999 along came Pope John Paul II to St. Louis. He personally asked Missouri's governor to pardon an inmate soon to die; and in his teaching, as well as in the revision of the *Catechism*, he has taken us, on the universal level, where our diocesan priests and religious wished us to go.

Priests also need to be engaged with issues larger than the merely parochial and diocesan. We need to allow them opportunities to engage in the lively debate of issues that we bishops have an opportunity to enjoy from time to time. Various sabbatical programs are available for priests, as are opportunities to learn from programs such as the National Pastoral Life Center of Msgr. Phil Murnion, the National Federation of Priests' Councils, and the various professional groups in the Church—all provide an opportunity for the bishop and his priests to become greater "men of the Church."

Finally, I recall with a better appreciation a phrase Pope John Paul II once used, I believe, with the clergy of Rome. He said, in an extemporaneous aside, "*Parochus super Petram.*" He certainly was not establishing a new hierarchical order in the Church; rather, he was acknowledging that in the lives of Christian women and men, their pastor often stands first in their hearts and minds, above the pope and even above the bishop. I remind my priests from time to time that not everyone can always remember who the pope is, who the bishop is, what kind of job either is doing, or even how these men directly or indirectly affect their individual lives as Catholic Christians—but everyone knows who their pastor is. It is an important reality for every bishop in dealing with his priests.

I admire more each day those of my brothers who have borne the heat of the day, who lead and have led their local churches for a decade or more. Where they have been particularly successful, it has almost invariably been accomplished with a genuine sense of partnership in ministry with the priests of the diocese.

I hope to continue to perfect that partnership in my episcopal ministry.

PASTORAL CHARITY ROOTED IN PRIESTLY FRATERNITY

His Eminence Francis Cardinal George, OMI
Archbishop of Chicago

Often during the pastoral visitation of a parish, a bishop hears comments about the priest who is pastor. Some parishioners will comment negatively about various aspects of a priest's ministry: he can't preach well, he's a poor administrator, he doesn't agree with the complaining lay person. But then, quite often, the parishioner will remark that Father is nevertheless a "good priest." When the bishop asks what that means, the response is usually, "Bishop, he loves us."

Jesus instructed St. Peter to feed his flock because Peter loved Jesus himself (cf. Jn 21:15-17). But loving the Lord entails loving those whom the Lord gives to Peter's care; and when a bishop hears that people recognize a pastor's love for them, he knows that the Church, both pastors and people, continues to recognize what it means to pastor in the name and with the authority of the risen Lord.

In the last generation, the Church has promulgated two very significant documents on the ordained priesthood. The first, *Presbyterorum Ordinis* (*Decree on the Ministry and Life of Priests*) of the Second Vatican Council, was released in 1965.[1] The second, *Pastores Dabo Vobis* (*I Will Give You Shepherds*), the post-synodal apostolic exhortation of Pope John Paul II, was released in 1992.[2] Both the Council's decree on the priesthood and the Holy Father's apostolic exhortation offer a wealth of perspectives and insights about the ministerial priesthood. In this essay I would like to focus on one important aspect of their teaching on priesthood: pastoral charity. I propose to examine the concept, situate it in the broader context of the Church's teaching on priesthood, and, most important for my purpose here, explicate the intrinsic connection between priestly fraternity and the authentic exercise of pastoral charity in the life of a priest.

PASTORAL CHARITY

In *Pastores Dabo Vobis,* the pope writes extensively on pastoral charity, describing it as "the internal principle, the force which animates and guides the spiritual life of the priest."[3] Some commentators have observed that, because of the frequency of the term's use in the exhortation (the term "pastoral charity" appears approximately thirty times and is present in each of the document's chapters) and because of the term's use to describe the identity, activity, and spirituality of the priesthood, the Holy Father has synthesized the Church's understanding of priesthood, drawing together into a coherent whole the various components of priestly life and spirituality. The pope's novel, repeated, and insistent use of the term makes it one of the important contributions of *Pastores Dabo Vobis* to the Church's understanding of the ordained priesthood.

At first blush, it may seem strange to call "pastoral charity" a new or important contribution to the Church's teaching on priesthood. Has it not always been part of the Church's Tradition—going all the way back to the post-resurrection exchange between Jesus and Peter—that love is connected to leadership of Christ's flock (cf. Jn 21:15-17)? St. Augustine referred to the priesthood as an *amoris officium*. How then can the concept of "pastoral charity" be seen as a contemporary development or contribution to our understanding of priesthood?

While charity in the exercise of priestly ministry has always been promoted in church teaching, the specific formula of "pastoral charity" is largely absent in church teaching prior to the Council. Papal teaching on priesthood prior to the Council emphasized priestly zeal, greater love in the care of souls, and the "bond of perfection" that unifies a priest's life. These strands are synthesized in the formula "pastoral charity" that was revived at the Council and subsequently developed by Pope John Paul II.

Pastoral charity is mentioned seven times in conciliar documents: once in *Lumen Gentium* in reference to bishops, and six times in *Presbyterorum Ordinis* in reference to priests. Although the repeated, formulaic use of the notion of pastoral charity in *Pastores Dabo Vobis* represents a flowering or development in the Church's understanding of priesthood, it does not represent a departure from tradition; rather, it gathers and synthesizes the tradition, giving it new expression and focus.

In reaction to the Holy Father's teaching that pastoral charity has its specific source in the sacrament of Holy Orders,[4] one might object that *all* Christians are called to a life of charity and that the virtue of charity is one and indivisible. Although this is true, it is nevertheless legitimate to allow for nuance and coloration in the one virtue of charity. The love shared between spouses, for example, is different in purpose, color, tone, and intensity from the love shared between neighbors. The love between spouses finds its foundation and meaning in the sacrament of Matrimony, which gives it a different accent than love shared between people who are not spouses.

In a similar way, the love that priests have for the Church, the flock entrusted to their care, is rooted in the sacrament of Orders, which shapes and determines the meaning and expression of that love. Pastoral charity must be understood within the context of the Church's teaching on the sacrament of Orders. In other words, it must be understood theologically.

In our culture, influenced as it is by the social sciences, there is the temptation to begin with the psychological and to understand realities like love only in psychological terms. Though the virtue of charity certainly has affective dimensions, it is first and foremost a faith reality. Its origin is in Christ. To approach it only from an affective, psychological perspective is to reduce it and rob it of its richness and its deep roots in a life of faith. Important though the warmth and personal care that a priest shows to the flock entrusted to him is, pastoral charity as a virtue is a participation, through the sacrament of Orders, in Christ's own love for his Church.

The Holy Father states that "by sacramental consecration the priest is configured to Jesus Christ as Head and Shepherd of the Church," and that "the spiritual life of the priest is marked, molded and characterized by the way of thinking and acting proper to Jesus Christ, Head and Shepherd of the Church, and which are summed up in his pastoral charity."[5] Here he offers an important key for understanding the specific nature of pastoral charity: the Headship of Jesus Christ.

HEADSHIP OF CHRIST

The conciliar documents stress in various ways the connection between the ministerial priesthood and the Headship of Christ. *Lumen Gentium*, paragraph 28, states that priests exercise "the office of Christ, the Shepherd and Head."[6] *Presbyterorum Ordinis*, paragraph 2, develops this theme of headship and states that, through the sacrament of Orders, priests "are configured to Christ the priest in such a way that they are able to act in the person of Christ the head." Other sections of the same document describe priests as "servants of the Head"[7] and as exercising "the function of Christ as Pastor and Head."[8] In *Pastores Dabo Vobis*, Pope John Paul II picks up this idea and makes the sacramental configuration of priests to Christ the Head one of the central themes of the entire document.

The notion of headship is rooted in a sacramental understanding of the Church as the Body of Christ. A body must be connected with its head in order to have life. Christ's Headship over his Body, the Church, is the foundation for communion and mission in the Church. Through the sacrament of Orders, ordained priests, members of the Body, become instruments of Christ's Headship. Through the ministry of priests, Christ, the Head of the Church, gathers all the members of the Body under his Headship. Both the Council's decree on priesthood and the Holy Father's apostolic exhortation affirm that, although all Christians through Baptism are incorporated into the Body of Christ as members, the ordained priest represents Christ precisely as Head.

Although all the baptized participate in Christ's relationship to the Father through sanctifying grace, the ordained priest participates also in Christ's relationship to the Church, his Body and his Spouse. That participation is the grace specific to the ordained priesthood. Because the priest is a sacramental sign of Christ the Head, he is called to embody the Headship of Christ in his own life. This can be done only in the context of the priest's self-sacrifice in service of Christ's people. Both the Council's teaching and that of the Holy Father connect the Headship of Christ with his servanthood. Thus the authority associated with headship is not authority as conventionally understood outside of the context of faith. Rather, as the Holy Father stresses, it is an authority that can only be expressed as service because Jesus is "the 'Head' in the new and unique sense of being a 'servant.'"[9]

Pope John Paul II uses the Pauline notion of *kenosis* to give fuller resonance to the meaning of Christ's service and to demonstrate its radical nature as an obedient service that "attains its fullest expression in his death on the Cross."[10] Self-sacrificing obedience and service, then, are the salient characteristics of Christ's authority that is expressed in the notion of headship. The authority of Jesus coincides with his obedience to the Father, his service, and his *kenotic* gift of himself in sacrifice for our salvation. This is the context that governs any understanding of Christ's exercise of headship over the Church.

Christ's Headship over his Body, the Church, as understood in terms of his radically obedient service-unto-death, has profound implications for an authentic understanding of the sacrament of Orders as a configuration to Christ the Head. Through ordination, the priest becomes a sacramental representative of Christ the Head. Christ, not the priest, is the Head of his Body, the Church. But through sacramental ordination the priest represents Christ in his Headship and participates personally in that Headship. The ordained priest lives from the dynamic of Christ's relation to his Church.

For Pope John Paul II, pastoral charity is what ensures fidelity in the priest's representing to and for the Church her Head, Jesus Christ. The Holy Father describes pastoral charity as "the force which animates and guides the spiritual life of the priest inasmuch as he is configured to Christ the Head and Shepherd."[11] He describes the "essential content" of pastoral charity as "*the gift of self, the total gift of self to the Church*, following the example of Christ."[12] Quoting one of his own homilies, the pope continues, "Pastoral charity is the virtue by which we imitate Christ in his selfgiving and service. It is not just what we do, but our gift of self, which manifests Christ's love for his flock. Pastoral charity determines our way of thinking and acting, our way of relating to people. It makes special demands on us. . . ."[13] Pastoral charity is therefore both a gift of the Spirit and a task and call to be lived; it is a constitutive part of both the structure and dynamic of the sacrament of Orders.

The Church's understanding of pastoral charity resists an individualistic interpretation. It is a temptation, especially in the United States, to take an individualistic approach to ordained priesthood, to see it as a personal honor or position of personal power or an office based on personal expertise. Such an understanding of priesthood is not only personally corrupting for the priest but also leads to a provincialism or parochialism in mission that is at odds with what the Church teaches about priesthood being at the service of the mission of the whole Church.

Just as a husband marries for the sake of his wife, a priest is ordained for the sake of the Church. Both marriage and orders are social sacraments, essentially implicating others. A priest is ordained with a title of service to a local church if he is a diocesan priest, or to a mission given by the Church to a community of consecrated life. This new relationship of configuration to Christ, the Head of the Church, therefore places the priest in relationship to a presbyterate, an apostolic community of faith and mission.

PRIESTLY FRATERNITY

One of the great recoveries of the Second Vatican Council was a renewed emphasis on the local presbyterate as integral to priestly identity and a source of priestly spirituality. Although the importance of the presbyterate—the body of ordained priests gathered around the bishop to assist him in making visible Christ's Headship of the local church—eroded through the centuries and gave rise to a more individualistic notion of priesthood, the Council revived the sense of a prebyteral college and reasserted its importance in the ministry and lives of priests.

In *Pastores Dabo Vobis,* the pope affirms the conciliar vision of the ordained priesthood as a collective reality, an order in the Church. While asserting that a priest's fundamental relationship is to Jesus Christ,[14] the Holy Father also holds that "it is within the Church's mystery, as a mystery of Trinitarian communion in missionary tension, that every Christian identity is revealed, and likewise the specific identity of the priest and his ministry."[15] He then goes on to describe this fundamentally relational dimension of priestly identity with ecclesial communion: "the priest sacramentally enters into communion with the Bishop and with other priests, in order to serve the people of God who are the Church."[16] Building on the Council's vision, Pope John Paul II grounds his understanding of the priesthood in what has been called a "trinitarian ecclesiology," which understands the Church as mystery, communion, and mission.

Because the Church is to "relive the very *communion* of God" and "manifest it and communicate it in history," Christ gathered around him the twelve, conferring on them "special powers" for the sake of continuing the Church's mission. These "Apostles, appointed by the Lord, progressively carried out their mission by calling . . . other men as Bishops, as priests and as deacons, in order to fulfill the command of the Risen Jesus who sent them forth to all people in every age."[17] Configuration to the Headship of Christ in the sacrament of Orders makes the priest a member of the presbyterate, constituting his priesthood as a reality relational to Christ, to the Church, and to his brother priests.

The presbyterate is to be understood in this wider context of *communio*. The sacrament of Orders initiates the priest into the presbyterate, an apostolic community of faith for the sake of priestly mission. Every ordained priest exists not in isolation but in relation to the apostolic community of mission comprising his bishop and brother priests.

Priestly fraternity, then, is not a "nice" thing to create or a good disposition to have; nor is it primarily for the sake of friendship. Rather, it is a constitutive dimension of the sacrament of Orders, intrinsic to the very mission a priest receives in ordination. In this context of membership in the presbyteral order, "priests are called to prolong the presence of Christ, the One High Priest, embodying his way of life and making him visible in the midst of the flock entrusted to their care."[18] Pastoral charity is the internal principle of priesthood, allowing priests to make Christ's love present because they live it in their hearts and souls, but this pastoral charity will be grounded and reflected in priestly fraternity made visible in the presbyterate.

PASTORAL CHARITY AND PRIESTLY FRATERNITY: PRACTICAL CONSIDERATIONS

If the sacrament of Orders configures a priest to Christ the Head, inserts him into an apostolic community of faith and mission (the presbyterate), and bestows on him the grace of pastoral charity as both a gift given and a call to be lived, then it must be in the visible priestly fraternity that a priest will best be able to respond to the call to live out the pastoral charity of Christ for the sake of the Church's mission. This belief has practical implications for the "living out" of priesthood. Like pastoral charity, priestly fraternity is both a gift given in ordination and a task to be lived throughout the life of a priest.

A number of practical obstacles impede the development of fraternity among priests. Perhaps most obvious is the diminished number of priests. More and more priests are living alone. The days of three and four priests in rectories, at least in large dioceses with built-in opportunities for fraternity, are for the most part past. The busy-ness of most priests' lives is another obstacle. Funerals, weddings, communion calls, counseling, teaching, meetings—all absorb time and energy, making it more of a challenge to find ways to develop relationships with other priests. A third obstacle is an excessive parochialism. Some priests refuse to look beyond the boundaries of their own parish and so lack a larger vision of presbyterate and Church; they forget that they were ordained for the Church and not for a parish created by the Church.

A challenge, as well, to the development of bonds of fraternity is the diversity of backgrounds—both ethnic and otherwise—that men now bring with them into the priesthood. The seminary experience of belonging to a particular class based on one's year of ordination often shaped and fostered bonds of fraternity among seminarians in a diocese, bonds that lasted into the priesthood. This sense of class identity is weakened. Because of the extraordinary variety of backgrounds, there is not the "natural" cohesion within a class today that there often used to be in larger dioceses. This is not of itself a bad thing. Diversity of backgrounds among priests is a blessing for the Church; but fostering fraternity must then become more intentional and challenging. Men often leave seminaries today without a deep sense of commitment to their classmates, and this lack can translate into isolation from other priests after ordination.

Although there are many practical obstacles to fostering fraternity, it is crucial for priests to be committed to fraternity and to find ways of moving towards living it effectively. The mission of the Church depends on their fraternity—and pastoral charity demands priestly fraternity. The Council's decree on priesthood offers some concrete suggestions for strengthening the bonds among priests. Building on them, I would like to suggest three ways to foster this spirit of fraternity for the sake of mission: presence, prayer, and partnership.

Presence

Priests need to find ways to be present to each other. Many obstacles work against such presence; but if priests are serious about the common nature of the mission they share as priests, presence to one another on a regular basis is essential. This presence can take many forms: dinners, days off, and convocations; periodic meetings of priests in a cluster or deanery; retreats together; common planning of services and pooling of pastoral resources. Whatever the context may be, fraternity will not develop without this kind of deliberate regular presence. Again, fraternity is not in the first place about friendship, though that may be a happy byproduct. It is primarily about the Church's mission and priests' sharing in that mission with each other.

Prayer

Presence is not always physical or visible. Time spent before the Blessed Sacrament praying for other priests brings a priest's brothers deeply into his life, even if he seldom sees them. Prayer with and for each other is essential for the kind of fraternity required of priests through ordination.

Priestly spirituality also seeks time when priests can be physically together in prayer. Just because diocesan priests are not members of a religious order does not preclude a life of prayer together. It can take many shapes, and experimentation may be necessary. Some prayer together is crucial, because the mission priests serve is not simply about the tasks they perform, but about representing the presence of Christ the Head to his Body. Collectively, priests should be present to him in prayer. They're gathered around Christ the High Priest. Priests' conversations among themselves must include conversations with Christ—with whom, in whom, and through whom they convene with one another. The Council's restoration of the practice of concelebrating the Eucharist is of a piece with the Council's teaching on the ordained priesthood. Ideological objections to concelebrants are, deliberately or not, attacks on the priesthood itself. They reduce ordained priesthood to a service for the congregation immediately before him.

Partnership

Finally, a sense of partnership is essential to developing bonds of priestly fraternity. A "lone ranger" mentality diminishes the status of ordained priesthood. Even if a priest lives alone in a parish, a sense of partnership in mission with fellow priests reminds him that he does not minister and live in isolation but as part of the presbyterate for the Church. Again, collaboration on common projects can help to forge and foster this sense of partnership. Clustering in deaneries or vicariates to plan events and further the spiritual renewal of both priests and people is one way to make partnership in ministry part of a priest's life.

CONCLUSION

Presence, prayer, and partnership are essential for strengthening the bonds of brotherhood that are at the heart of priestly ministry and spirituality. In ordaining priests, the Church calls upon the Holy Spirit to configure them to Christ the Head of the Church, giving them the capacity to participate in Christ's own pastoral love for his flock. The "essential content" of pastoral charity is the "gift of self" to the Church. Pastoral charity is at the service of the Church's mission, a mission that has been particularly entrusted to priests who serve it in the context of priestly fraternity. For the sake of the mission, for the sake of representing and embodying the pastoral charity of Jesus Christ for all his people, priests work to deepen and strengthen the bonds of fraternity among themselves. Without this fraternity, the mission is weakened and pastoral charity diminished.

St. Peter was one of the twelve, the head of the apostolic college commissioned by the Lord himself. Peter was not only given a flock to love as Christ would love them, but he was also given brothers to love as colleagues in a common mission. Today, as two thousand years ago, pastoral charity and priestly fraternity create the context for every priest's life and ministry.

NOTES

1   Second Vatican Council, *Presbyterorum Ordinis* (PO) (*Decree on the Ministry and Life of Priests*). In Austin Flannery, ed., *Vatican Council II: The Conciliar and Post Conciliar Documents*, new rev. ed. (Northport, N.Y.: Costello Publishing Company, 1996).

2   John Paul II, *Pastores Dabo Vobis* (PDV) (*I Will Give You Shepherds*) (Washington, D.C.: United States Catholic Conference, 1992).

3   Ibid., no. 23.

4   Cf. ibid.

5   Ibid., no. 21.

6   Second Vatican Council, *Lumen Gentium* (*Dogmatic Constitution on the Church*). In Flannery, op. cit.

7   PO, no. 12.

8   Ibid., no. 6.

9   PDV, no. 21.

10 Ibid.

11 Ibid., no. 23.

12 Ibid.

13 Ibid.

14 Cf. ibid., no. 16.

15 Ibid, no. 12.

16 Ibid.

17 Ibid., no. 15.

18 Ibid.

MINISTRY OF THE WORD, THE PRIMUM OFFICIUM OF THE PRIEST, AND THE "NEW EVANGELIZATION"

Most Reverend Charles J. Chaput, OFMCap
Archbishop of Denver

"WOE TO ME IF I DO NOT PREACH THE GOSPEL"

Let me begin with a simple suggestion: Example works. Unless we bishops are evangelizers in a direct and personal way, we can hardly expect our priests to be any different. Unless we place preaching the word of God first in our own vocation, whatever counsel we offer to our brothers in ministry will be fruitless. The priests we have in the new millennium will be determined by the bishops we are today. Our witness will set the tone. I'll return to this point at the end of these brief thoughts. But it's important to begin by recalling what all of us already know in our hearts: that any prescription we write for the behavior and attitude of our priests must apply first and with even more force to ourselves as bishops, or it will accomplish very little.

Presbyterorum Ordinis, echoing *Christus Dominus*, stresses that "since nobody can be saved who has not first believed, it is the first task of priests as coworkers of the bishops to preach the Gospel of God to all men."[1] Through preaching the Word, they "set up and increase the People of God,"[2] which is born "not from perishable but from imperishable seed, through the living and abiding word of God" (1 Pt 1:23). And since no one can give what he does not have himself, the Council urges priests to "immerse themselves in the Scriptures by constant sacred reading and diligent study,"[3] the better to nourish the seed of God's presence in their own hearts.

Every priest is configured to Jesus Christ by ordination; the first words we hear from the Lord's mouth in Mark are these: "This is the time of fulfillment. The kingdom of God is at hand. Repent, and believe in the gospel" (Mk 1:15). Christ preached always and everywhere, with an unmistakable urgency. The priest likewise is designed to be the sower of the seed of life, which is God's word. God's word has power. Nothing proves this more clearly today than the phenomenal growth of evangelical churches that—despite the incomplete nature of their message—announce the Gospel with confidence and enthusiasm. And it's no accident that churches that have lost their missionary zeal or softened the authority of Scripture are in decline. The lesson is sobering. This is why Paul says, "Woe to me if I do not preach [the Gospel]!" (1 Cor 9:16). His meaning is twofold.

First and more obviously, while all Christians have the duty to preach the Gospel, priests are the Word's special stewards. And, like the servants in the Parable of the Talents, we who are priests will be held more accountable in this missionary task than our people, for we are their shepherds. But second and more importantly, faith that is not shared dies. "Maintenance-mode" Christianity does not exist. Happiness for the priest depends on our bringing others to know Jesus Christ, and deepening the roots of the word in the hearts of those who already profess him. If priests do not live the ministry of the word ardently and actively, we cannot be happy, because we are made to be a model and sacrifice for others. We are made to witness.

In a sense, every priest already knows this. Few would dispute that interest in the Scriptures has grown tremendously throughout the Church since Vatican II. But while studying God's Word and preaching Jesus Christ are intimately linked, they are not the same things. I would argue that over the last thirty-five years, especially in the United States, the missionary character of priests has too often seemed muted. The proclamation of the word has suffered as a result, and too many people have not heard the Good News with the freshness and energy it deserves. Too many former Catholics now worship in the same evangelical churches that feed off the weaknesses of mainline Protestant traditions. For the Catholic faith to thrive in the new millennium, that needs to change.

THE NEW AREOPAGUS

Priests do not stand outside their culture. We are part of it. Understanding it, therefore, becomes an important part of examining our own ministry of the word and its challenges.

In regard to Scripture, my first point is this: We can't give our hearts to something that we believe needs fixing. Priests can't confidently preach a message that we suspect may be flawed or culturally conditioned. Critical distance diminishes love, in exactly the same way that a husband who habitually picks apart the perceived weaknesses of his wife will not stay married for very long. We already see this in too many of the internal controversies that unsettle the Church. We can love the Church if we see her as the Bride of Christ. We cannot love an "institution" that we feel needs restructuring according to one or another agenda.

In like manner, the methods we have applied to unpack the sacred texts for the past fifty years have provided us with many vital insights into the origins and context of God's word. The Church wisely encourages such research when it is conducted in a spirit of humility and faith. But these methods can also run the risk of separating us from the underlying integrity of the message. The debates over gender and biblical language have done this already. In deconstructing Scripture, we risk objectifying it and placing ourselves outside and above it. This can result in a kind of reductionism or dissection that kills life. A parallel example is the collapse of philosophy into linguistics at many universities. This has ensured that the secular academy is often too busy bickering over the meaning of questions to seriously pose the important ones.

The same kind of decomposition can occur in our approach to God's Word. The Good News is a seed, and a seed is a living thing, not a mechanism that we can disassemble and reassemble at will. Scripture is God talking to his people, but if we do not dispose ourselves toward listening for his voice, we will not hear. This is why *Dei Verbum* stresses that "prayer should accompany the reading of sacred Scripture, so that a dialogue takes place between God and man."[4] And the council fathers then quote Ambrose, who notes that "we speak to [God] when we pray; we listen to him when we read the divine oracles."[5] The *real* reality of Scripture—the living presence of God within the text—becomes clear only when we pray over it with our hearts. This applies just as forcefully to priests and bishops as to the lay faithful.

My second point is this: I believe too many of us among the clergy have in some ways misunderstood the meaning of the Council's call for *aggiornamento*. We who are priests need to be more courageous in our preaching and less concerned about the opinion of the world. As John Paul II writes in *Redemptoris Missio*, "All priests must have the mind and heart of missionaries,"[6] because "missionary evangelization . . . is the primary service which the Church can render to every individual and to all humanity in the modern world."[7]

Aggiornamento—opening ourselves to the world, listening to it and learning from it—does not imply being silent in the face of the world's sinfulness. The guiding star for every priest is his relationship with Jesus Christ, not his people or culture, *precisely because* he loves his flock. In fact, ministry to his flock will frequently require him to draw the distinction between the requirements of genuine Christian love and the much less demanding value of "tolerance."

Tolerance is a useful attribute for any society. But when it becomes an excuse for inaction or silence in the face of trends that undermine authentic human dignity, it becomes an obstacle to real pluralism. Real pluralism assumes that people of conviction will work to advance their beliefs by every legal and moral means at their disposal—wisely, respectfully, but nonetheless forcefully.

All law and all politics emerge from this struggle of convictions. By its very nature, the word of God creates in us a healthy unrest about the world. It bears fruit in convictions that have deep social consequences. This is why God's word is both loved and reviled. To preach Jesus Christ, but then to demur from advancing our views on unpopular issues, simply makes no sense. Priests are not immune to this temptation. In fact, in some ways we are particularly prone to it because of our daily encounter with people of drastically different sufferings and needs.

Silence in the face of sin or error, however, is never pastoral charity. It was the "tolerance" of the Areopagus (Acts 17:16-31) that made it uniquely resistant to the message of St. Paul. And I suspect John Paul II was thinking especially of the United States when he spoke of the "modern Areopagi" in *Crossing the Threshold of Hope*. He describes them therein as "the worlds of science, culture, and media . . . the worlds of writers and artists, the worlds where the intellectual elite are formed" that vigorously resist the Gospel in a "struggle for the soul of the contemporary world."[8]

My third and final point is this: On Pentecost, the apostles came out of the upper room consumed by the fire of the Holy Spirit and utterly confident in the word of God. They had neither the resources nor the personnel to change the world. But they did so on the power of the Word. Their preaching of Jesus Christ drew thousands. I agree that issues of resources and personnel are important. Burnout among our priests can be a serious concern. But resources gravitate to those who offer energy and hope. The rapid growth of renewal movements within the Church since Vatican II—movements that combine energy, piety, and exhilarating confidence in God's word—is a prime example.

The solution to our problems of priestly life is not simply an increase of "professionalism" among the clergy. The priesthood is not and can never be a job, though professional skills are very valuable. Rather, priesthood is an abandonment of oneself into God and his word—and when people see God genuinely transforming us, they will seek the same for themselves. People are hungry for more than the Areopagus provides. But they will only follow leaders they trust, and they will only trust leaders who radiate the joy of salvation and the power of the Word in their own lives.

THE WORD BECAME FLESH; THE WORD BECOMES FLESH

In *Pastores Dabo Vobis*, Pope John Paul II writes of "the absolute necessity that the 'new evangelization' have priests as its initial 'new evangelizers.'"[9] The "new" evangelization is more than a new label and a fresh marketing campaign for an old product—though, obviously, the basic mission of the Church never changes. The "new" evangelization is linked to the unique needs of the modern—or more accurately, postmodern—world. We are "overmedia-ed" and "under-truthed." In the Information Age, we too often lack the one piece of information that finally matters: the Word that is life.

The emerging global culture will be marked, at least in the early decades of the new millennium, by the character of American culture: pragmatic, materialistic, and self-assured; but also fragmented, privatized, deeply skeptical toward institutions and ideals, utilitarian, and caught between pride in our achievements and despair at the scope of our problems. Much of the western world may still *appear* to be Christian, but it's not—at least not in any real sense of the word "Christian." Rather, it is mission territory in need of a new generation of missionaries.

In his book *The Revolt of the Elites*, written shortly before he died, historian and social critic Christopher Lasch lamented the "gradual decay of religion" in the Western democracies, and noted that "the separation of Church and state, nowadays interpreted as prohibiting any public recognition of religion at all, is more deeply entrenched in America than anywhere else. Religion has been relegated to the sidelines of public debate."[10]

He continued by saying that "the elites' attitude to religion ranges from indifference to active hostility. It rests on a caricature of religious fundamentalism as a reactionary movement bent on reversing all the progressive measures achieved over the last three decades."[11] Moreover, "the vacuum left by secularization has been filled with a permissive culture that replaces the concept of sin with the concept of sickness."[12]

None of this would have seemed alien to St. Paul, preaching in the twilight of the Mediterranean's pagan religions. But it is new territory for Christians who once presumed at least the sympathy, if not outright encouragement, of civil culture toward their faith. This is why listening uncritically to the postmodern song is so imprudent—and why the tools of postmodern culture need to be used only with an alert mind and a vigilant eye on their side effects. As Neil Postman observed more than a decade ago in his essay

"Social Science as Moral Theology," we can learn a great deal from the "social sciences," but we would do well not to confuse them with real science. In fact, he argued, they are not science at all, but a form of storytelling, a particular kind of moral narrative.[13] Moreover—we might add—they have embedded biases that may, or may not, be friendly to religious faith.

The new evangelization therefore requires a serious rethinking of our entire relationship with the world. Too often in the past thirty-five years, our engagement and cooperation with the world have elided into assimilation, which has then become a matter of the world's simply digesting the Gospel without noticeable effect. The Word became flesh to change the world, to redeem and transform it—not to *be changed by* it.

The Word became flesh uniquely and unrepeatably in the person of Jesus Christ. The priest, configured to Christ, is called to be the Word *becoming* flesh again and again in the life of contemporary society. It's no accident that John Paul II, who so frequently has preached the need for the new evangelization, is also the pope who has had such an extraordinary interest in issues of culture. In my *Webster's New World Dictionary*, "culture" has six different definitions. Only the last three deal with the network of ideas and tastes that we commonly call culture. The first three, in contrast, have to do with the cultivation or nourishment of fields, plants, and living things.

It makes sense. Culture is organic; it grows from beliefs and habits the way a living shoot emerges naturally from a seed. When the Word becomes flesh in the lives of our priests, then the seed takes root in the lives of their people; and when it becomes flesh in the lives of our people, then it becomes culture—Christian culture. A culture of life.

It has always been so. Now more than ever, every priest must be a missionary priest; every seminary must be a missionary seminary. And the most practical step in accomplishing this is to become missionaries again, ourselves, as bishops. We are evangelizers first and managers second. We are preachers and teachers first, and ecclesial executives a distant second. When we can say honestly in our own vocations that this is so—when we can show through our own direct, personal witness what it means to be a "new evangelizer" and a minister of the Word—then the brothers who cooperate with us in our service to the People of God will follow.

NOTES

1 Second Vatican Council, *Presbyterorum Ordinis* (PO) (*Decree on the Ministry and Life of Priests*), no. 4; cf. Second Vatican Council, *Christus Dominus* (*Decree on the Pastoral Office of Bishops in the Church*), no. 12. In Austin Flannery, ed., *Vatican Council II: The Conciliar and Post Conciliar Documents*, new rev. ed. (Northport, N.Y.: Costello Publishing Company, 1996).

2 PO, no. 4.

3 Second Vatican Council, *Dei Verbum* (*Dogmatic Constitution on Divine Revelation*), no. 25. In Flannery, op. cit.

4 Ibid.

5 Cited in ibid.

6 John Paul II, *Redemptoris Missio* (*On the Permanent Validity of the Church's Missionary Mandate*) (Washington, D.C.: United States Catholic Conference, 1991), no. 67.

7 Ibid., no. 2.

8   John Paul II, *Crossing the Threshold of Hope* (New York: Knopf, 1994), pp. 112-113.

9   John Paul II, *Pastores Dabo Vobis* (*I Will Give You Shepherds*) (Washington, D.C.: United States Catholic Conference, 1992), no. 2.

10 Christopher Lasch, *The Revolt of the Elites and the Betrayal of Democracy* (New York: W. W. Norton, 1995), p. 215.

11 Ibid.

12 Ibid., p. 216.

13 Cf. Neil Postman, "Social Science as Moral Theology." In Neil Postman, *Conscientious Objections: Stirring Up Trouble About Language, Technology, and Education* (New York: Knopf, 1988), cf. pp. 5, 12-13, 16-18.

PREACHING THE GOSPEL IN THE NEW MILLENNIUM: OBSTACLES AND HOPES

His Eminence Roger M. Cardinal Mahony
Archbishop of Los Angeles

But how can they call on him in whom they
have not believed? And how can they believe
in him of whom they have not heard? And how
can they hear without someone to preach?
And how can people preach unless they are sent?

—ROM 10:14-15

To hear that a crisis of priestly identity exists in the Church today is not uncommon. Commentators and critics are quick to offer their reasons, but these are all too often based on a simplistic reading of a complex matter. Priestly identity can only be discerned within the context of priestly relationships—with Christ, the bishop, other priests, and the priestly People of God. Understanding the priesthood principally in terms of what the priest does reflects a fundamental misunderstanding of the meaning of priests' true identity and of the sacrament of Holy Orders. It is, then, a source of deep regret that some priests have so overly identified with what they do that when others take up tasks previously reserved to them or when they retire from their ministry, they are disoriented and despondent; they no longer know who they are. If our identity rests upon what we do, then personal crisis is likely to occur eventually. If we have no deep personal and spiritual resources to sustain us, then we will have little to rely upon when we have little or nothing to do. In short, if we are what we do, then when we don't, we are not!

THE PRIEST'S MINISTRY AS EVANGELIZATION

The Parable of the Sower (Lk 8:4-8) conveys a message about different kinds of soil for proclaiming and receiving the word. Even though some are not congenial to the seed of God's word, we must nonetheless sow continually. The parable challenges the priest to probe more deeply the grace of preaching that lies at the core of his vocation to ordained ministry. For preaching the Gospel is not merely one of the priest's tasks among others. It is not just a piece or part of the priest's ministry—another thing to be done, albeit a very important task. Rather, the ministry of the priest *is* evangelization, in that the priest is to proclaim the Gospel with the entirety of his life in relationship to Christ, the bishop, his brother priests, deacons, and the priestly People of God. Within the context of priestly relationships, priestly ministry is properly understood *as* evangelization—a way of *being* over *doing* in service of the Gospel of Jesus Christ, hope of the world.

The unique constellation of the ordained priest's participation in the ministry of Christ takes the following three forms: (1) witnessing to the Word, (2) sanctification through sacramental celebration, and (3) exercising pastoral leadership. The priest builds up the Church through this threefold ministry. What is particularly distinctive about the ministry of the priest is the charism and office of sanctification. Those ordained to the priesthood are to be holy men called to lead the People of God in the fundamental Christian vocation of witness, worship, and service. However, since the first responsibility of the priest as co-worker of the bishop is to "preach the Gospel of God to all,"[1] the office of witnessing to the word is prior to the office of sanctification. Preaching is not limited to the liturgical homily, though that is its focus. It includes the evangelization that precedes and follows worship, as well as the teaching that accompanies it.[2] The priest's way of holiness through the grace of sanctification is in and through the proclamation of the Gospel—the exercise of his entire ministry *as* evangelization.

A reason to hope (cf. 1 Pt 3:15) for the effective proclamation of the Gospel in the new millennium lies in the recovery of an understanding of priestly ministry *as* evangelization within the context of priestly relationships—with Christ, the bishop, brother priests, and the priestly People of God. This calls for a deep conversion to the word of God, a willingness to ponder the word long and lovingly, giving flesh to the word not just in words but in a whole way of life. It is only as we respond to the grace of contemplative prayer, attending to the Word beneath and beyond all words, that we will be able to pass on to others the Good News of the Living Word through the ministry of witness to the word, sanctification through sacramental celebration, and pastoral guidance and leadership.

Each of us must face a hard question: Do we, in fact, see the gift and the task of evangelization as our top priority? Have we set our hearts on evangelizing our people, or are we inclined to think that because they are "sacramentalized" they are evangelized? Have we taught our people, but not evangelized them? Does our teaching in matters of doctrine and morality, central as it is, sufficiently take into account that people today do not readily receive this teaching as Good News? Have we yet come to terms with just how pressing is the need for pre-evangelization? How do we teach in such a way as to help people of many different cultures and languages who are listening to us—sometimes all at once—hear the Gospel as Good News?

In his post-synodal apostolic exhortation *Ecclesia in America*, Pope John Paul II speaks of evangelization repeatedly in terms of a fresh encounter with Jesus Christ.[3] While most priests today recognize that "the Church" is the People of God—all of them—for countless people in today's world, "the Church" means "the priests" or "the hierarchy." Do others, within the Church and beyond, know us to be men who have had such a "fresh encounter" with Christ, an encounter that is expressed in a "witness of actions"?[4]

One of the central challenges of the Gospel is to make the values of the kingdom our own, and then to live them out in the midst of a world that does not choose or even value them. We are to be yeast in the dough, to be countercultural, to swim against those currents antithetical to the Gospel. Our task is not to "please the folks." Preaching the Gospel often demands that we speak a hard word. But even as we do so, we are to reconcile God's people, remaining approachable and open, collaborative and supportive of all those truly seeking the common good. Indeed our whole "tone of being" should be good news, even as we speak a hard word.

If we are to take up the task of a "new evangelization" or "re-evangelization"—"new in ardor, methods and expression"[5]—then perhaps we should admit that we need to set aside those duties and tasks that encumber us from fulfilling this central role. Such an admission clears a way for an increase of hope—the hope proclaimed in the Gospel of Jesus Christ whose heralds we are.

How well do all the activities of the priest relate to the principal task of evangelization? In what ways do they drain priests of the energy and the passion for what is first and final in the priestly ministry: the proclamation of the Gospel for the hope of the world? And I think that this question must be asked: In what ways might we have allowed these various activities to become a substitute for our ministry of evangelization?

If ours is to teach, preach, sanctify, and guide *as* a proclamation of the Good News, we would do well to consider this: What are those elements that "dog" us in the exercise of our ministry? What things have accrued to the ordained ministry, those dreaded issues that may not be as central to it as we are inclined to think? When considering the reworking of our priorities that I am suggesting, where would we place concerns such as parish personnel decisions, fund raising for very worthy projects, and those seemingly endless meetings? In the face of these issues and others like them, have we unwittingly allowed ourselves to become parish CEOs, administrators, and managers of parochial complexes large and small?

It is not my intention here to suggest which of our many tasks might need to be set aside. But it is important to see all that we do in service of that which is first and finally the task of the priest: to preach the Gospel. In such a perspective, some things may indeed have to be set aside, given up, or delegated to others who may be more gifted for a particular task than we are. Giving up what is not our principal task *can* liberate us for the service of the Gospel.

OBSTACLES AND OPPORTUNITIES

In every age, elements of culture may be congenial to the proclamation of the Gospel, or they may pose obstacles. We do not stand outside or above culture. Even as we raise a prophetic voice in the face of those cultural currents that are antithetical to the Gospel, we must recognize the influence of cultural factors both positive and negative in our own lives. The ministry of evangelization requires that we not underestimate the seriousness and the gravity of the obstacles, cultural and personal, to the effective proclamation of the Gospel. These must be reckoned with and examined closely. However, despite them all, the preacher continues to be optimistic because of the virtue of Christian hope.

Certainly the Parable of the Sower conveys the message that some soil, be it cultural or personal, is not good ground for the reception and cultivation of the word. But in considering the ministry of evangelization, if we envision the culture as consisting of one obstacle after another, a range of elements hostile to the Gospel, does that not put us in a position of constant nay-saying to the world in which we live? And if we say "no" to the culture in which we live, must we not say a resounding "yes" to another way of perceiving and being, ourselves becoming embodiments of what we preach: a "yes" that is borne out through a witness of actions in our proclamation of Christ Crucified and Risen, the hope of all?

It might be more helpful for us to consider the obstacles to the proclamation of the Gospel more in terms of *mixed* and *ambiguous* reactions to the Gospel, rather than as obstacles that render the culture and those affected by it altogether hostile to the Good News. It may be even more accurate to say that we live in a culture that is *indifferent* to the Gospel. If this is so, then what is required is a considerably different approach to evangelization from that which is called for if the culture is conceived of as hostile, ridden with one obstacle after another.

It is far too easy to paint a picture of the United States in broad strokes of depravity, debauchery, and decadence—a culture completely at odds with the Gospel, the Church, and her ministers. More nuances are not merely desirable, but required, if we are to respond to the gift and the task of evangelization. What is needed is sharper discernment, more appreciation for light and shadows, as well as darkness. How to sift wheat from chaff? In the face of certain developments in science and technology, cultural fragmentation, and the widening gap between rich and poor, the priest must always work in concrete ways to make the message of the Gospel known and heard.

Several features of our culture, usually thought of as creating obstacles to the Gospel, call for deeper discernment.

First, a culture of material plenty is positive or neutral, and has certain advantages. Abundance may be a blessing from God. But this must be judged in light of the gap between rich and poor, and in view of the fact that today the acquisition of material abundance is driven by a consumerism that impoverishes millions.

Second, a culture of opportunity, with a strong affirmation of individual rights and liberties, is not negative per se. But the unbridled individualism and opportunism in some cultural currents undermines the importance of solidarity as cogently articulated by Pope John Paul II, and works at cross-purposes with the pursuit of the common good.

Third, a culture with a strong commitment to safeguard the freedom of the human person is a good. But in our culture the rhetoric of freedom of choice has muted the rhetoric of commitment to, and responsibility for, others.

Fourth, tolerance, democratic process, consultation, participation, and accountability are values that few of us would be willing to jettison, even though they can cause tension, and at times conflict, with the "culture" of the Church. They cannot be dismissed outright as obstacles to the Gospel, even though at times they manifest themselves as suspicion of authority of any sort, reluctance to give obedience to anyone, or reticence in the face of any claims of truth or universal norms.

These and other features of our culture call for greater discernment. But there are two elements that I see as clearly antithetical to the Gospel. The first is the low esteem for human life, increasingly apparent in our culture, which is greatly at odds with the riches of our heritage. Our culture is certainly "unwelcoming soil" for a word of life that safeguards the dignity of each human person created in the image of God—a word in defense of the wounded and the weak, the last, the littlest, and the least.

The second element that creates unwelcoming soil is materialistic consumerism. Pope John Paul II likens its effects to the results of Marxism, Nazism, and Fascism, as well as to the effects of such myths as racial superiority, nationalism, and ethnic exclusivism. "*No less pernicious* [emphasis mine], though not always as obvious, are the effects of materialistic consumerism, in which the exaltation of the individual and the selfish satisfaction of personal aspirations become the ultimate goal of life."[6]

CHALLENGES YET TO BE MET

It is a very simplistic reading of a complex situation to say that the obstacles to the proclamation of the Gospel brought on by indifference or even hostility are the result of deeply embedded cultural factors. Could it be, rather, that many are indifferent to the Church and its ministers because the saving message of the Gospel has not been taught in a way that really *gives life*, in a way that helps our people make sense out of their lives and loves, inviting and encouraging them to live with just a bit more hope and a clearer sense of the future?

In our ministry of preaching we rely on very familiar words: the language of sin, grace, salvation, redemption, resurrection. Indeed we should. But do we speak this language in a way that helps others comprehend the meaning of our words? How might the rhetoric of our proclamation ring out as Good News to those who are actually poor and homeless, to the single parent, to a young person with a chronic illness?

Our proclamation of the Gospel should help our people live the joys and delights of human life in the presence of the divine, to see and to celebrate all that they have as gifts through and through. We need to find more effective ways to help our people to be and to build the Body of Christ in and for the world. We cannot assume any longer that because they are catechized and sacramentalized they are evangelized. If we see the task of preaching as moral exhortation or imparting of doctrine on one hand, or boosting the morale of the assembly on the other, then much of our religious and theological language will become "semantically empty," lacking real meaning for our people. Unless we rise to the challenge of preaching a word that gives life, it should come as no surprise that those in the culture remain indifferent to the Gospel, or that those within the Church grow increasingly indifferent as well.

In the face of indifference, the hope for effective evangelization rests in presenting an argument that is persuasive of the message. Making a persuasive case for the Gospel does not mean "selling Jesus" in the marketplace, "dumbing down" the Gospel, or making it more palatable to the "spiritually hungry" in our consumerist culture. Rather, if we are to persuade others of the veracity of the claims of the Gospel, then we must ourselves be persuaded of the plausibility of our claims. If this is so, then we may need to penetrate more deeply what we seek to pass on to others: the Word of Life. Amidst many pressing demands, we ourselves may need to make yet more time for sustained theological reflection, for scriptural study, and for greater familiarity with the spiritual and mystical heritage of our tradition. Or we may need to rely on the help of those more knowledgeable than ourselves in these crucial areas. Indeed we need a fuller comprehension of the truths we proclaim, even as we admit that certain truths are not within our grasp, are beyond our comprehension.

Are we sufficiently knowledgeable about Sacred Scripture, tradition, and church teaching, and sufficiently persuaded of the truth expressed therein to proclaim it cogently and persuasively to our people rather than simply being prepared to defend it? Are we content to teach what the Church teaches simply because the Church teaches it? If so, how can this possibly be Good News for those who are indifferent to the Gospel, the Church, and its ministers?

If the culture is thought to be hostile to the Gospel, then we may be inclined to think that a firm hand or a sharp voice is the proper strategy. But if the culture is just plain indifferent, then the only chance of getting through is with a message at once precise and persuasive, rooted in a personal praxis of the Gospel. Christ's saving word and work must be borne out in the priest's personal witness to the truth he proclaims. Recall the words of Pope Paul VI in *Evangelii Nuntiandi*: "As we said recently to a group of lay people, 'Modern man listens more willingly to witnesses than to teachers, and if he does listen to teachers, it is because they are witnesses.'"[7]

By sacramental ordination, the priest is to proclaim the Gospel with the whole of his life through the ministry of witness to the word, sanctification, and pastoral guidance and leadership of the faithful. The entirety of his person is to be a saving word, a saving work. Indeed, his way of being should be an offer of grace, of God's gift, calling all within the Church and beyond it to a radically new way of perceiving and being. The priest is to be a sign, indeed a sacrament, of the Gospel, evoking from others the fullness of life in Christ. He is to be a herald of hope.

Three elements in the contemporary culture have wounded us deeply: individualism, pragmatism, and restlessness.[8] Indeed these factors pose very serious obstacles to proclaiming and living the Good News of Christ.

One of the governing concerns of our culture is safeguarding the rights and liberties of the individual. Added to this is the conviction that the individual is capable of giving shape to his or her life and destiny through personal choice from among a seemingly infinite range of options. We are inclined to think of persons, ourselves and others, as individuated centers of consciousness. We strive mightily for self-sufficiency and self-determination as if these were the principal goods of human life and development. In such a perspective, we are individuals before we are a community. We are selves prior to being in communion with others. This view is fundamentally at odds with an understanding of the human person created in the *imago Dei*, created with the capacity for relationship with another, others, and God, and such a view lends itself all too easily to self-preoccupation, self-absorption, self-fixation. Briefly, our culture cultivates individualism and breeds narcissism.

We are a highly pragmatic people. This has its advantages, to be sure. We work hard. We try to be efficient. We want to get things done. But the flipside of this is that we tend to be overly concerned with results, with outcomes we can measure and assess. So many of us are impatient with theories and ideas. We deplore ivory tower speculation. In our culture, the truth is what works. And if it works it must be true. We say "the proof is in the pudding." We judge persons by what they do. We value people because of their achievements. But this tendency poses a real difficulty in our response to live by the grace of Christ, because the gift of God's love in Christ will not succumb to our instruments of assessment. The Christian life authentically lived is a most impractical thing to do. Imagine priests rising in the hours before dawn to ponder long and lovingly over the word of God! What's the use? What good does that do?

In addition to breeding narcissism and bottom-line pragmatism, our culture gives rise to another obstacle: unrelenting restlessness. We are hungry for experience. We want to go places, see things, do things. The refrain heard all too frequently these days says it all: "Been there, done that." So we move on to the next thing. Our lives are filled with cacophony and clutter. In most of our homes, the television is our constant companion. We "channel surf" through an ever-expanding menu designed to please our viewing appetites. Our attention span seems to decrease as our digital options increase. We are afraid to be alone, still. We cannot seem to stay in one place. Even while walking in the park or by the lake or sea, we fill our ears with music or the news or a trashy talk show via portable radios.

Today there is a growing realization that these elements of our culture pose serious obstacles to the fullness of human and Christian life. And it is increasingly recognized that these factors, so prevalent in the culture at large, have also gained a firm foothold in ecclesial life as well.

The culture that breeds narcissism, pragmatism, and restlessness is a dead end. Whatever the gains of modern culture, its toll on persons, communities, and nations has been enormous. People today are beginning to realize that a culture built upon the pillars of pragmatism does not, in fact, hold up in the long run. It cannot endure. It has been found wanting. Modern culture has not made good on its promise. It has failed to satisfy the deepest desires of the human heart and has resulted in fragmentation and depersonalization of a magnitude previously unimagined. People are looking for another way.

PRIESTLY MINISTRY: A WAY THROUGH THE OBSTACLES

The ordained priest heralds hope for a new way of perceiving and being that is altogether antithetical to the individualism, pragmatism, and restlessness of our age.

The priest cannot understand himself first and foremost as an individual. Rather, the priest is who he is and does what he does in and through his relationship with Christ, the bishop, other priests, and the priestly People of God. His identity is necessarily trinitarian and ecclesial—that is, relational. The ministerial priesthood is situated in a set of relationships: within the trinitarian communion, with bishops, with laity, with the Church, and with the world. In a word, the ordained priesthood is fundamentally a relational reality; it is radically communitarian. As priests interiorize this profoundly spiritual and theological foundation of their relational identity, their ministry and mission will become a source of hope for those caught in the dead-end of self-absorption and self-fixation—the rotten fruit of the culture of individualism.

What is distinctive about the ministry of the ordained priest is the charism and office of sanctification. How is this ministry of sanctification best exercised? We sanctify not only through the administration of the sacraments, but also by the quality of our presence, our pastoral charity and compassion for a people who, living among the world's many problems and difficulties in their daily lives, are subject in a particular way to anxiety and suffering.

For our sacramental ministrations to be Good News, to be a fruitful exercise of the ministry of sanctification, we ought to find a stable sacramental ministry within the eucharistic community of faith and worship. This entails much more than saying Mass and hearing confessions in the same parish. It calls for much more than accomplishing a seemingly endless number of pastoral tasks within the parish boundaries. I am suggesting that priests actually become engaged in a living community of faith, hope, and love so as to take up, perhaps for the first time, an ongoing and vibrant sacramental ministry with a people waiting to hear the proclamation of the Gospel as Good News.

As we take up the many duties that occupy us as priests, do we allow ourselves the opportunity to enter into relationship with a particular community in its prayer, worship, pastoral need, and pastoral outreach? Should we not draw from the wisdom of our people, listening to their voices at prayer and in pain, sharing their pastoral initiatives, allowing their experience to inform our efforts at evangelization?

The profoundly relational and communitarian identity of the priest is expressed through his ongoing sacramental ministry in a community to which he really belongs. This may become increasingly difficult as more and more priests become responsible for more than one parish—and in some cases, several parishes. But this should not obscure the truth that it is within the context of ecclesial relations that our people might come to know us as the men we really are, as the priests Christ has called for witnessing to the word, for sacramental ministry, and for pastoral leadership and guidance. Within the context of a fuller understanding of relationship between the priest and the priestly People of God, there might arise new expressions and methods for our ministry of evangelization, shaped by ongoing participation in the life and worship of a particular people, and in response to their pastoral needs. Perhaps this kind of ongoing participation would challenge us in unprecedented and unforeseen ways to speak a word of life through and through, to "interpret the human situation through the Scriptures,"[9] keeping the message fresh week by week, moving even a heart frozen by indifference to respond to the promise and the hope that is Christ.

The entirety of the priest's ministry can be a proclamation of Good News, depending on how it is exercised. This is especially true of the manner in which the priest guides and leads. The priest represents Christ in his headship. But he is nonetheless part of a pilgrim people, a people on the way, probing paths of virtue and holiness. The priest stirs hope for the Good News in those who are indifferent when he cultivates in word and deed those dispositions of spirit that render him an effective sign of ecclesial relationship, a sacrament of the holy communion that is the Church. In cultivating dispositions of spirit such as patient listening, respect for others, confidence, and humility, the priest becomes a countercultural witness, announcing the Gospel of God to all, a God whose very being is to be in relationship.

Preaching the Gospel as a whole way of life is a most impractical thing to do. It has ever been thus. In the earliest days of the Christian community, Paul boldly proclaimed that the Gospel is a stumbling block, foolishness, but that God's foolishness is wiser than human wisdom (cf. 1 Cor 1:18). In the culture at large, as well as within the Church, there are enormous pressures to be efficient and effective, to achieve realizable goals, and to assess the outcomes of our projects and planning. We are reminded constantly that parishioners want to hear meaningful homilies that speak to their concerns, words that touch their hearts and minds. They long for a form of liturgy that fills their spiritual hunger. All of these factors may have the effect of sending the priest into pragmatic overdrive, working hard to find the right technique for delivering the meaningful and compelling homily, and striving mightily to celebrate the sacraments in just the right way so that they "work" for people.

In the face of such pressures, the priest must recognize that he is not ordained to produce results or to achieve precise outcomes. We cannot easily assess the outcomes of the Christian life. Indeed, there is no "bottom line" to the Word of Life, who is boundless and bottomless love pouring forth endlessly and eternally.

The priest is part of the pilgrim people. Like every human heart, his is restless until it rests in God. But rooted in the Living Word of God, the priest's life gives hope to those driven by unbridled restlessness because he knows the One he is seeking. Year by year, season by season, week by week, day by day he is washed in the ebb and flow of the Word of God. As others race from this thing to that, looking for the experience that will satisfy their spiritual craving, the priest's call is to sink in deep down, cultivating, nurturing, and sustaining roots long, deep, and strong in the Word of God. This can only be done if we devote ourselves to the regular discipline of sacred reading, to the slow, careful, contemplative pondering of the Word of God in Scripture. Too often, priests approach the Word of God in a fundamentalist manner. Further, they often approach Scripture with a pragmatic, utilitarian frame of mind: "What can I get out of the Scripture that will help me give a good homily?" While the priest should always have his ministry of preaching in mind while reading, indeed contemplating, the Scripture, the word of God is not to be thought of principally in terms of its usefulness. Far too often Scripture is used to bolster the point of a homily. But the art of preaching does not consist of making a point through moral exhortation or doctrinal exposition. The art and craft of preaching lie in breaking open the word, allowing the Living Word beneath the words to stand forth. Even as the preacher seeks to express the Word of God in and through the words of the homily, it must be recognized that these words are in service of the Word beneath and beyond all our words. But how are we to serve the Living Word of God in this way if we do not find our stability, our ground, in Scripture itself? Further, how are we to offer hope to a people driven by unrelenting restlessness if we are not at rest in the word of God, the proclamation of which is our prime ministry as priests?

PRIEST AS HERALD OF HOPE

If the priestly ministry is to be exercised *as* evangelization, then what is called for is not another preaching technique or homiletic method. What is required, not merely desired, is the sustained discipline to become a herald of hope in the face of the individualism, pragmatism, and restlessness that are so much at odds with the message of the Gospel. But unless this hope is embodied in our own living of a countercultural message of ecclesial relations— seeking the true and valuable over the useful, staying still long enough to listen long and lovingly to the Living Word of God beneath the words—we will have little or nothing to offer a people earnestly seeking a way through the obstacles, both cultural and personal, to the fullness of life, light, and love.

When we commit ourselves again and again to the lifelong discipline of priestly ministry *as* evangelization we stand a better chance of allowing the Word beneath the words to stand forth in the liturgical homily. As we are embraced by the Word through a life of ecclesial relations, our preaching can become more deeply attentive to the needs of the hearers of the Word who gather

Sunday after Sunday to celebrate Christ's mysteries in word and sacrament in the Church's liturgy. As we grow in our knowledge of Scripture by sustained pondering of the Word, we will be impelled to proclaim its truth in season and out of season as an expression of our faith and love[10] of Christ, the Incarnate Word of God, rendered present in our preaching.[11]

Hope for preaching the Gospel amidst the obstacles that must be faced in the new millennium rests in seeing our entire life and ministry *as* evangelization, in becoming heralds of hope in word and deed.

If we take up our ministry in the ways I have described, I am convinced that we have some chance of breaking through the massive walls of indifference, offering others reasons to hope. Our people know in their marrow that the individualism, pragmatism, and restlessness of our day have no future. These trends result in bankruptcy of spirit, causing a crisis of hope. The people look to us for another way—of ecclesial relations, speaking the truth in love, at rest in the Word of bottomless love pouring itself forth.

In the face of obstacles that at times appear beyond counting, the priest is to announce the Gospel for the hope of the world. But what exactly is the hope to be preached in word and in deed through priestly ministry? Without a firm understanding of this oft-neglected virtue, we may be ill-prepared to give an account of the reasons for the hope that is within us (cf. 1 Pt 3:15), especially in the face of indifference.

Hope is the very center of a human being, the drawing force of all human initiative. It looks to the coming of the new, the never before, the undreamt of. Hope is a movement of the person by which we relativize the present and all its prospects of success so as to be open to something that we realize can only come as gift.

The more unpromising the situation in which we demonstrate hope, the deeper the hope is. Hope is precisely what we have when we do not have something. Hope is not the same thing as optimism that things will go our way, or will turn out well. It is rather the certainty that something makes sense, is worth the cost, regardless of how it might turn out—even if there are no positive outcomes! Hope is a sense of the possible. It strains ahead, seeking a way behind and beyond every dead end.

Hope is directed to a future good that is hard but not impossible to attain. But its attainment is in the mode of reception, because hope is an openness to possibility that can only come as gift—letting something that is not self-generated come into life.

But with this gift comes judgment. The counterpart of hope is the admission of shortcomings, indeed of failure, despite our noblest intentions. Such an admission makes room for the Spirit's coming in the gift of hope. Indeed hope of the deepest kind calls for humility, a willingness to allow ourselves to be judged by the Gospel, to submit to its apocalyptic sting. But it is not simply our culture with its obstacles that needs to be judged by the Lordship of Christ. At times it is also our own exercise of the ordained ministry that for many people, both inside and outside the Church, is not a reason for hope, but instead is a reason for indifference and, at times, hostility. This is a necessary step in responding with a full heart to the challenge of the new evangelization.

Finally, recall that the Parable of the Sower conveys a message about different kinds of soil, or environments, for the word. Just because some of these are indifferent or hostile to sowing the seed of God's word does not absolve us of the effort to sow continually. The parable is intended as a message of hope to the preacher—not to be discouraged. If hope in Christ gives any assurance it is this: The more difficult the circumstances, the greater the challenge to hope.

If we are to be more effective servants of the Gospel for the hope of the world, we must cultivate, nurture, and sustain the hope that lies within us before we can stir it anew in others. Hope is never achieved alone. Its attainment, which is always in the mode of reception, occurs in the context of relationship to Christ, and to the members of His Body, the Church. Perhaps the Parable of the Sower challenges the priest in his relationship to Christ, his bishop, other priests, and the priestly People of God to create more opportunities to help one another and learn from one another in the work of evangelization.

The whole Church, the Body and all its members, is responsible for evangelization. Without this realization, and without creating the conditions for all the baptized to take up their proper task in the work of evangelization, the ministry of the ordained priest will not be as fruitful as it might be. Creating opportunities for the priest to work together with the priestly People of God to find ways of together proclaiming the Good News is part of the pre-evangelization required by the new evangelization—new in ardor, methods, and expression—and is a necessary step if priests in this new millennium are to exercise our ministry *as* evangelization.

NOTES

1   Second Vatican Council, *Presbyterorum Ordinis* (*Decree on the Ministry and Life of Priests*), no. 4. In Austin Flannery, ed., *Vatican Council II: The Conciliar and Post Conciliar Documents,* new rev. ed. (Northport, N.Y.: Costello Publishing Company, 1996).

2   Cf. Second Vatican Council, *Sacrosanctum Concilium* (*Constitution on the Sacred Liturgy*), no. 9. In Flannery, op. cit.

3   John Paul II, *Ecclesial in America* (EA) (*The Church in America*) (Washington, D.C.: United States Catholic Conference, 1999), no. 7 and passim.

4   John Paul II, *Centesimus Annus* (*On the Hundredth Anniversary of Rerum Novarum*) (Washington, D.C.: United States Catholic Conference, 1991), no. 57.

5   John Paul II, Address to CELAM, Port-au-Prince (March 9, 1983); *Redemptoris Missio* (*On the Permanent Validity of the Church's Missionary Mandate*) (Washington, D.C.: United States Catholic Conference, 1991), no. 33; *Tertio Millennio Adveniente* (*On the Coming of the Third Millennium*) (Washington, D.C.: United States Catholic Conference, 1994), no. 38; EA, chapter 6.

6   John Paul II, *Respect for Human Rights: The Secret of True Peace* (Washington, D.C.: United States Catholic Conference, 1999), no. 2.

7   Paul VI, Address to the Members of the *Consilium de Laicis* (October 2, 1974). Cited in Paul VI, *Evangelii Nuntiandi* (EN) (*On Evangelization in the Modern World*) (Washington, D.C.: United States Catholic Conference, 1975), no. 41.

8   Pope John Paul II focuses on individualism and its consequences as a major obstacle to the Gospel in nos. 6-10 of *Pastores Dabo Vobis* (*I Will Give You Shepherds*) (Washington, D.C.: United States Catholic Conference, 1992).

9   Bishops' Committee on Priestly Life and Ministry, National Conference of Catholic Bishops, *Fulfilled in Your Hearing: The Homily in the Sunday Assembly* (Washington, D.C.: United States Catholic Conference, 1982), p. 20.

10 Cf. EN, nos. 76, 79.

11 Cf. Paul VI, *Mysterium Fidei* (*On the Holy Eucharist*) (Washington, D.C.: National Catholic Welfare Conference, 1965), no. 36.

THE ROLE OF PRIESTS IN CATECHESIS IN THE NEW MILLENNIUM: ANCHORED IN TRADITION

Most Reverend Donald W. Wuerl, STD
Bishop of Pittsburgh

In the long Tradition of the Church, there have been many attempts to describe the specific work of the priest. One effort took its inspiration from St. Paul's description of his ministry as he tried to be "all things to all" (1 Cor 9:22). The Church in her liturgy and pastoral office speaks of the threefold task of the priest: to teach, to lead, and to sanctify.

At different times, different aspects of this threefold ministry have received more emphasis than others. Not long ago priesthood was depicted almost entirely in terms of sacramental ministry and, specifically, the celebration of the Eucharist. The priest as steward of the sacred mysteries (cf. 1 Cor 4:1) was recognizable at the altar, in the Anointing of the Sick, in the confessional, or while preparing people for the sacraments, especially Matrimony.

In the early years of the Church in our own country, the leadership role of the priest was particularly important. He was the recognized leader and spokesman for the faithful—many of whom had only recently come to this land. While clearly the "steward of the mysteries" of Christ, the priest was also the leader of God's people as their builder, guide, organizer, and counselor.

The leadership and sanctifying roles of the priest certainly continue even though they may find expression in an expanded context. Nonetheless, today there is a need to focus on the priest's prophetic ministry. As the new century dawns, a difficult work faces us—one for which this world has little patience and even less interest: the prophetic task of proclaiming the call to faith in God, to life in his name, and to the kingdom to come.

The need for catechetical renewal in our country highlights the imperative of a more explicit teaching of the faith. We refer to the "lost generation," "religious illiteracy," and "catechetical deficiencies" as a way of expressing the diminished level of intellectual awareness of and personal loyalty to the revealed teaching of Christ and its application that we refer to as the "received tradition."

The faithful who sit in the pews around us at Sunday Mass have not all had the advantage of continuous religious instruction as they grew up and developed intellectually and spiritually. Today, the majority of the generation passing on the faith to their own children did not themselves learn of it from the consecrated women and men who were once so prominent in Catholic schools. They may have had only sporadic, superficial instruction in the faith, leaving them with little foundation for addressing the issues of life, including life's purpose for themselves and their children.

Our culture is aggressively secular and often hostile to Christian faith. The social mores, particularly as seen in large urban centers and reflected in the means of social communication that reach our entire country, are almost entirely focused on the material world. Commentators often speak of a generation that has lost its "moral compass."

At the same time, we see a disintegration of those community and social structures that once supported religious faith and encouraged family life. The heavy emphasis on the individual and his or her rights has greatly eroded the concept of the common good and its ability to call people to something beyond themselves. When the individual is the starting point, the result is a diminished awareness of the intrinsic value of others and even a temptation to see others as objects or means to an end. In this setting, their value is determined only by what they can "do for me."

We experience this in our society and in the law, for example, when one person's right to life falls victim to another person's right to privacy. This conflict has a strong impact on the capacity of some to accept a teaching that is revealed by God and not decided by democratic vote, or to follow an absolute moral imperative despite its inconvenience or unpopularity.

Our proclamation of the Good News of Jesus Christ and the teaching of his Church is met by the "American mindset" that is more individual than communal, more competitive than cooperative, and more self-serving than self-giving. It is no wonder that many of our faithful feel uncomfortable with a Church that identifies herself as a community whose source is Christ and that preexists the decision of its individual members to bring it into being—a

Church whose teaching binds consciences to follow Christ's teaching, and a Church that requires its members to come together in order to praise God and challenges them at the same time that it comforts them.

In the use of the word "community," for example, many Americans automatically assume a gathering of like-minded individuals from the same economic group, or what Robert N. Bellah refers to in *Habits of the Heart* as "lifestyle enclaves."[1] The community of Christ's Church, however, is Catholic—a radically inclusive assembly made up of both friends and strangers, fellow citizens and "foreigners," all standing before the face of God in worship and mutual acceptance.

When we hear the claim that a number of Catholics do not accept the Church's teaching—whether on abortion, euthanasia, capital punishment, marriage, sexuality, racism, societal care for the poor, or some other moral issue—we need continually to remind ourselves that there is a clearly articulated body of Catholic teaching. At the same time, we need to recall that the faith is not forced on anyone. It must be freely embraced and generously lived. This can only happen if there is someone to proclaim fully, clearly, and convincingly God's word and the teaching of Christ. Bringing Jesus into our lives includes acceptance of the teaching of Christ's Church as the voice of Christ himself. "Whoever listens to you," Jesus said to his apostles, "listens to me" (Lk 10:16).

"Is living together wrong if the couple intends to get married?"

"Why can't I have an abortion if this pregnancy is so inconvenient to me and my future plans?"

"Why shouldn't I cheat when everyone else does?"

"What is wrong with lying if it helps me get ahead?"

The answers to these and many similar questions come either from our faith or the culture around us, which looks elsewhere for its inspiration.

In his preaching and teaching, the priest needs to be the counter-cultural voice that offers sound and sure answers to life's questions. These responses derive from the Church's Tradition—the millennia of reflection on the human condition under the guidance of the Holy Spirit. While these responses may not always be popular, they are true. They lead us to God. Like John the Baptist, who pointed and proclaimed, "Behold, the Lamb of God" (Jn 1:29), so the priest needs to point to Christ, his way, his teaching, his Gospel in a world that all too readily does not see him in the midst of all the other alternatives.

Many in pastoral ministry recognize a new openness to God and the things of the Spirit among our young people. There is a sense among them that the secular, material world does not provide them with sufficient answers for their lives. Over and over, the phenomena of youth gatherings as large as World Youth Day or as small as some parish programs reveal the search for meaning, value, and direction that characterizes what is in the hearts and minds of a growing number of our young faithful. There is a hunger for God that we need to encourage, inform, and satisfy.

The Priestly Prophetic Voice

At the heart of a Catholic's response to the guidance of the Church is the faith conviction that Jesus has not abandoned us to whatever current of political correctness blows across society on any given day. We live in the assurance that Jesus cares for us and walks with us in the form of the Church, our Mother and Teacher. In searching for sure footing on our pilgrimage through life, we come to realize that, as Jesus told us, the wisdom of the Church is heard in the voices of those who speak for it.

We priests must proclaim Jesus to be the way, the truth, and the life. While not everyone always lives up to the challenge Christ sets before us, we must make sure that they at least know what that challenge is. To fail to measure up to the truth is one thing; to be uninformed about it is entirely another.

The priest has to be the voice and the presence of the Church's teaching ministry in action precisely because the acceptance of the teaching authority of the Church, as exercised by bishops and the priests in union with the bishops throughout the world, is a "hard saying." The *Catechism of the Catholic Church* has devoted a large section to this teaching function.[2]

The recent instruction from the Congregation for the Clergy, *The Priest and the Third Christian Millennium: Teacher of the Word, Minister of the Sacraments, and Leader of the Community*, reminds us of the teaching of the Second Vatican Council's decree *Presbyterorum Ordinis*: "It is the first task of priests as co-workers of the bishops to preach the Gospel of God to all. . . ."[3]

The *General Directory for Catechesis*, published in 1997 by the Congregation for the Clergy,[4] is intended as a tool to complement the *Catechism of the Catholic Church* as we address the new evangelization. The *Directory* reminds us that this is a new moment in the life of the Church precisely because we are called upon to see our teaching ministry in the context of the new evangelization. Our Holy Father, Pope John Paul II, has repeatedly challenged us to reach out to those who have drifted away from the practice of the faith or who were never sufficiently catechized.

Most of us experience in our pastoral ministry the mingling of both the initial proclamation and ongoing catechesis, and the blurring of lines that would clearly identify stages of development in the appropriation of the faith. Too often the people we are dealing with catechetically, while perhaps sacramentally already initiated into the Church, are still in some stage of entering for the first time into a personal encounter with God and are still in the process of coming to believe in Christ.

We often encounter young parents who, when called to be the first teachers of their children in the ways of the faith, experience their own first serious personal catechesis as they share in the catechetical programs for their children. While this is far from the ideal, let us not lament but accept this as a second chance for both them and us. The "new evangelization" unfolds on two levels simultaneously: the introduction of the faith to very young children, and the instruction of their parents. For both catechists and those already catechized, this moment can be particularly enriching as these young adults approach the faith with a great deal more openness and out of their own felt need to know more.

The priest is prophet and pastor. He stands in the midst of the faith community as the good shepherd whose voice is recognized as that of Christ. For this reason, his proclamation of the truth from the pulpit is balanced by his compassionate care of the flock when they come for counseling and sacramental confession. These two dimensions of priestly service are components of effective ministry.

When he knows his flock, the priest can speak the word of God in ways that can arouse them to life-giving love and lead them to Christ. The pastor-prophet teaches against abortion and at the same time offers forgiveness to those who have had one. He proclaims the indissolubility of marriage and attempts to hold onto and draw into the embrace of the Church one who has suffered marital breakdown and married again outside the Church. The good shepherd must call for peace and forgiveness and also encourage and guide those who do the work of public order.

The priest, as shepherd and prophet, can neither guide in the ways of the truth nor heal what has been broken by isolating or separating these two aspects of the same rich, Christ-like ministry. From the pulpit the priest must proclaim the truth—the complete and unvarnished truth—that is the way to salvation. As confessor, counselor, and spiritual guide, the priest as shepherd must meet the members of his flock where they are in order to support and walk with them on their pilgrimage to the Father.

In the New Testament, the followers of Jesus marveled that unlike other teachers he taught with authority. In Matthew's Gospel, we read, "Now when Jesus finished these words, the crowds were astonished at his teaching, for he taught them as one having authority, and not as their scribes" (Mt 7:28-29). The authority of Jesus was rooted in his identity: "I am the way and the truth and the life," he proclaimed (Jn 14:6). The truth, the very reality of who Jesus is, is what he shares with us in and through his Church.

In his post-synodal apostolic exhortation *Ecclesia in America*, Pope John Paul II reminds us that our encounter with Christ begins with conversion.[5] The priest stands in the midst of the faith community as one who introduces the believer to Christ, helps the believer to deepen a relationship with the Lord, and continually proclaims the way that we who walk with Jesus are to follow.

It is not an exaggeration when the Church says that as the priest proclaims the teaching of the Church, he speaks with the voice of Christ. This is what priestly prophetic ministry is about today.

OUR MINISTRY ANCHORED IN TRADITION

Where do we, as the prophetic voice of Christ, turn to find the message we are to proclaim? We do not preach about ourselves but rather about Christ and his crucifixion. We authenticate our proclamation by our continuity with the crucified Christ in and through the Church. It is in the apostolic Tradition or handing on of the message that we find not only the source of what we proclaim but also its authentication. Continuity with the apostolic ministry of the Church is what confirms our own personal proclamation and gives reason for our hearers to place their hope in what we say.

The revelation of God in Jesus Christ continues to come to us in and through the Church. Just as the word of God was spread through the efforts of the apostles, so too it is necessary that the word of God continues to be taught through the teaching and proclamation of today's apostles: the bishops and their principal collaborators, the priests. The Church is called "apostolic" precisely because the teaching of the Church is rooted in and is an articulation of the teaching of Christ that has come to us from the apostles.

Christ remains the teacher of his people. He continues to free us from the despair of ignorance and doubt, from the frightening fear that nothing makes sense: "For this I was born and for this I came into the world, to testify to the truth" (Jn 18:37).

Jesus continues to teach through those whom he sends. Priests are sent in Christ's name, in the name of the Church. The reason we can be confident of the truth of what we teach is that we are one with—

in communion with—the teaching of the whole Church, authenticated by the bishops together with our Holy Father, the pope. When we realize that our communion in teaching with the whole Church is communion with Christ's life-giving truth, we recognize the awesome responsibility that has been placed in our hands.

Our faithful people look to the priest, in the pulpit and in any teaching setting, to be a transparent proclamation of what the Church holds out for all people as the Tradition received from the apostles. The faith that comes to us from the apostles is our warrant for daring to stand in the midst of God's people and offer them words of everlasting life. No one can claim this of himself. It comes from another: Christ through the apostles in his Church.

Priests and bishops are servants of the word of God and as such have an awesome responsibility to be faithful to it so that those who hear it from us can accept what we teach with serene confidence. As public figures in the Church charged to present Christ's salvific plan, we, too, can rejoice in the assurance that what we teach does not come from us but from the Church that Jesus guaranteed would not fall into error.

How else would Christ's words—their meaning and their application—be passed on generation after generation, century after century, once he was no longer with us in the flesh, if there were not those who could articulate his will with the assurance that they were guided by his Holy Spirit?

What we have to say will often be countercultural, just as Jesus' message was. As we have already reflected, this is an age that does not draw its inspiration from gospel values. When our Holy Father, Pope John Paul II, speaks in *Evangelium Vitae* (*The Gospel of Life*) of the clash between a culture of death and a civilization of love, he sums up the struggle between two great visions of humanity reflected in our culture and in so much of our national public policy.[6]

SOME PRACTICAL SUGGESTIONS

The Priest and the Third Christian Millennium highlights the role of the priest as teacher of the Word. It reminds us that the preaching of the priest is his first and principal means of exercising his prophetic office in the Church. But it also goes on to remind us that the effective proclamation of the word as an expression of the new evangelization "demands a zealous ministry of the Word which is complete and well-founded. It should have a clear theological, spiritual, liturgical and moral content, while bearing in mind the needs of those men and women whom it must reach."[7]

The pulpit will retain its privileged position for the priest. It is from here that Sunday after Sunday we have an opportunity to directly touch our people in a way that nothing else we do can. I once read a statistic that on any Sunday throughout this land there are more people in churches listening to their priest or minister than there are attending all of the major sports events in the course of a year. Every priest has hundreds or even thousands of hearers each Sunday. We must not squander this gift.

The homily can be a graced moment to share the faith. The great, living, apostolic Tradition is ours to pass on to a generation that longs to be part of something good, life-giving, and meaningful. There was a time when moralizing dominated homilies. Today, the challenge the priest faces is to use the homily not only to encourage his flock in the practice of the faith but also to share with them the faith itself, the very content—the life-giving reality—of God's word.

THE ROLE OF PRIESTS IN CATECHESIS IN THE NEW MILLENNIUM • 123

The three-year cycle for the *Lectionary* provides us with an opportunity when integrated with the *Catechism of the Catholic Church* to touch on every aspect of our faith in a way that roots it in Scripture and relates it to our daily life. The *Catechism of the Catholic Church* is an extraordinary resource to couple with the *Lectionary* and our daily experience as we attempt to mold a homily that touches mind and heart.

All of us priests must find other ways and times to teach—to speak *of* Christ, to speak *for* Christ. This can happen in a hospital room, in a funeral home, at a family table. We are regularly asked to speak at what seems like countless events—parish, local, regional, and sometimes national. Each of these occasions can be an opportunity to teach the faith. No occasion lacks a spiritual dimension, for no place is foreign to the Gospel. The reason we are asked to say something at such events is to bring a spiritual dimension to the occasion. In my own experience, I have found that a brief reflection on some element of our faith is not only welcome but also greatly appreciated. The communication possibilities are almost endless: parish newsletters, websites, even bulletins can be effective teaching instruments.

I see many parish bulletins with a "pastor's corner," in which some teaching of the Church is highlighted effectively. Given the number of bulletins that are prepared and passed out every week, it seems a lost opportunity if the content is confined to the dates and places of various parish events. A pastor once told me that a parishioner came to him to obtain some additional reading material on the Eucharist because, in the words of the parishioner, "The small bulletin piece on the real presence was the first time I remember in recent times hearing about that aspect of our faith."

Precisely because we are priests, we need to take very seriously our responsibility of oversight for what is taught in the name of Christ.

The root of the word *episcopus* is "overseer." I try to discharge my responsibility through the establishment of catechetical policies and teaching guidelines for our schools and religious education programs. A pastor of a parish has the same obligation: to know what is being taught and to work with the teachers—particularly in light of the rich and useful materials recently provided by the Holy See and our own national bishops' conference. The *Catechism of the Catholic Church* is the universal norm against which our teaching can be measured. In this way, we can ensure a "common language" of the faith, taught in every tongue.

In addition to overseeing, supervising, and directing those who teach, a priest himself needs to take time to teach—to share the message in the RCIA, in adult and parent programs, as well as in classes for our young members. This cannot be left entirely to others, for by his participation in the teaching task, the priest confirms and validates the role of others to share in the prophetic work of Christ.

It is a truism that one leads by example. This is a moment in the life of the Church when the ministry of teaching needs to be highlighted in both word and deed so that all of our faithful people—particularly those engaged in the teaching ministry—feel that they are truly participating in a significant ministry of the Church. We priests need to turn as much attention individually to catechetical renewal today as we did to liturgical renewal in the late sixties and early seventies.

CONCLUSION

I want to add a word of encouragement. Often priests rightly feel that they are being asked to undertake one more project, one more program, one more activity, which is to be added to an already unachievable list of expectations. I do not believe that is true of the call to exercise our teaching ministry. Teaching is at the heart of who we are. Our faithful look to us to see Christ and to hear on our lips the teaching of his Church because it is there that we find the words of life.

Just as Jesus was able to preach with confidence and authority because of who he was, so too each of us, bishops and priests, can preach with assurance because of who we are: ministers of the Gospel in communion with an apostolic Tradition that reaches back to the very person of Jesus Christ.

NOTES

1   Cf. Robert N. Bellah, *Habits of the Heart: Individualism and Commitment in American Life* (Berkeley: University of California Press, 1985).

2   Cf. *Catechism of the Catholic Church*, 2nd ed. (Washington, D.C.: United States Catholic Conference, 2000).

3   Second Vatican Council, *Presbyterorum Ordinis* (*Decree on the Ministry and Life of Priests*), no. 4. Cited in Congregation for the Clergy, *The Priest and the Third Christian Millennium: Teacher of the Word, Minister of the Sacraments, and Leader of the Community* (Washington, D.C.: United States Catholic Conference, 1999), chapter 2, no. 1.

4   Cf. Congregation for the Clergy, *General Directory for Catechesis* (Washington, D.C.: United States Catholic Conference, 1997).

5   John Paul II, *Ecclesia in America* (*The Church in America*) (Washington, D.C.: United States Catholic Conference, 1999).

6   John Paul II, *Evangelium Vitae* (*The Gospel of Life*) (Washington, D.C.: United States Catholic Conference, 1995).

7   *The Priest and the Third Christian Millennium*, op. cit., chapter 2, no. 2.

THE ROLE OF THE PRIEST IN FOSTERING THE MINISTRY AND SERVICE OF LAITY IN THE CHURCH AND THE WORLD

Most Reverend Howard J. Hubbard
Bishop of Albany

Recently, I presided at a liturgy commemorating the 150th anniversary of a parish in the Diocese of Albany. The entrance procession contained twenty-four banners representing the various lay ministries being exercised currently in that particular parish community. I was struck by the fact that if a similar format had been employed on the occasion of the parish's centenary, at most five or six banners would have been carried in procession. Hence, this jubilee procession brought home very vividly and tangibly the explosion of lay ministries in our Church since the Second Vatican Council.

This growth of lay ministry, witness, and service is evident in so many ways. In the liturgical life of the Church, lay persons proclaim the scriptural lessons, serve as cantors and musicians, act as ministers of hospitality and extraordinary ministers of the Eucharist, and in some places are responsible for leading Sunday worship in the absence of a priest. All of the liturgical rites have been revised to provide for a more active participation by the worshiping community, and the implementation of the restored Rite of

Christian Initiation of Adults requires that lay persons fill many roles to enable it to work effectively.

The most dynamic spiritual renewal movements in the last few decades have been led and often initiated by lay persons, such as Cursillo, Charismatic Renewal, Marriage Encounter, Foculare, youth ministry movements, ministry to divorced and separated Catholics, bereavement support, and other similar groups. Along with their traditional involvement as catechists in the faith formation of children, youths, and adults, lay persons are being called upon to expand their activity as evangelization becomes a more explicit aspect of the Church's mission.

In many parishes, dioceses, and church agencies, lay persons have the opportunity to contribute to policy and decision making through structures like parish/pastoral councils, liturgy and faith formation committees, boards for finance and education, boards of directors of health care and social service agencies, Catholic conferences, and ecumenical committees.

Lay persons are being hired for full- and part-time positions on parish and diocesan staffs, especially in the areas of faith formation, youth ministry, liturgy, business administration, and social action, as well as in pastoral care to specialized groups like the elderly or those who are developmentally disabled. To prepare for these roles, a growing number of lay persons are seeking graduate degrees in theology and ministry and completing certification processes to acquire the skills and knowledge for these ministries.

In addition, innumerable lay persons now interpret their daily lives and responsibilities in family, business, civic community, neighborhood, school, interest groups, and culture as occasions for ministry, for Christian witness, for evangelization, and for living their faith actively in the world.

The experience of the past thirty years also indicates that the rise of lay ministry actions and services only begets further lay activity. By modeling lay ministry, by sharing their stories of being called to ministry, and by inviting others to an awareness of the spirit in their lives, lay men and women have been a wonderful resource for recruiting, supporting, and affirming other laity in the acceptance of new roles and responsibilities. For example, many of the laity who have completed ministry formation programs have enabled others to serve in a variety of ways:

- as leaders of priest retreats
- as leaders of small faith-sharing and scripture study groups
- as participants in AIDS care teams and retreat teams for those in jails and prisons
- as lay persons sharing their professional expertise with those in the wider community in activities such as counseling the unemployed, assisting immigrants with legal problems and language skills, and offering medical and nursing care in parish or school-based programs

All of these efforts seem to be responsive to the signs of the times: to the deep hunger for spirituality and a deeper understanding of the Scriptures; to the declining number of ordained and vowed ministers; to the rising aspirations of women; to the growing dehumanization and depersonalization within our society; to the alienation and disaffiliation of Generation X; and to the widening gap between the haves and the have-nots within our society.

This development of the laity's role in the Church and society is based upon two fundamental insights enshrined in the Second Vatican Council. First, the Council emphasizes that we are called by the Church to ministry through the sacrament of Baptism. The laity "are by baptism made one body with Christ and are established among the people of God. They are in their own way made sharers in the priestly, prophetic, and kingly functions of Christ. They carry out their own part in the mission of the whole Christian people with respect to the Church and the world."[1] This call of the laity was captured well after the 1987 Synod of Bishops in Pope John Paul II's apostolic exhortation *Christifideles Laici* (nos. 20, 28) and was echoed by the bishops of the United States in *Called and Gifted for the Third Millennium*, which states that

> Through the sacraments of baptism, confirmation, and eucharist every Christian is called to participate actively and co-responsibly in the Church's mission of salvation in the world. Moreover, in those same sacraments, the Holy Spirit pours out gifts which make it possible for every Christian man and woman to assume different ministries and forms of service that complement one another and are for the good of all.[2]

All the baptized in the communion of the Church, then, share, in their own particular way, in the priestly, prophetic, and kingly office of Christ, as well as in the mission of preaching the Gospel.

The second fundamental insight articulated by the Second Vatican Council is that the laity's call to ministry, witness, and service is issued not by a pope, bishop, or priest but by the Lord: "The lay apostolate . . . is a participation in the saving mission of the Church itself. Through their baptism and confirmation, all are commissioned to that apostolate by the Lord Himself."[3]

Hence, the rapid development of lay ministry since the Second Vatican Council must not be perceived as a practical necessity imposed upon the Church by the declining number of vocations to the priesthood and religious life we have been experiencing of late, nor is it motivated by some kind of American desire to democratize the Church. Rather, this phenomenal growth is the inevitable result of the Council's renewed appreciation of the laity not as mere instruments of the hierarchy but as the People of God who are called to holiness and ministry and who possess personal charisms that empower them to contribute their part to the mission of the Church and the transformation of society.

The laity's call to ministry and service, in other words, is not to be seen as a luxury or concession but as the natural consequence of their right and responsibility to participate in Christ's saving mission and to use their gifts and talents to advance God's kingdom in our day.

Understandably, however, this expanding role of the laity—significant blessing that it has been, and great source of hope and promise for the future that it offers—could lead to a crisis of identity for priests. Deep in their hearts priests might be haunted by the question, "Am I important, and what is my role?" If, for example, the laity can exercise roles as spiritual directors, leaders of scripture study groups, liturgical planners, or pastoral administrators—areas that were previously the priests' exclusive domain—is it any wonder that the identity of priests might be blurred and their confidence shaken?

In reality, the ambiguity priests experience today may have been fostered unwittingly by the decrees of the Second Vatican Council. For example, the Council addressed itself extensively to the role of the bishop and the laity but offered few insights about the role of priests. While the Council's document *Presbyterorum Ordinis* (*Decree on the Ministry and Life of Priests*) said some fine things about the priesthood, it was definitely one of the minor decrees, and the Council did not develop a contemporary theology of priesthood. In fact, the council fathers seemed to take the priesthood for granted somewhat and did not see the necessity to address the matter at great length.

In hindsight, as Fr. M. Edward Hussey suggested in a 1988 conference on "U.S. Catholic Seminaries and Their Future," the recent decline in the number of priests and the present status of the priesthood are the natural and perhaps even inevitable result of the documents of the Second Vatican Council. What is needed today, then, is a more deeply developed theology of the priesthood in light of the Second Vatican Council's emphasis on the Church as the entire Christian community, on the priesthood of all the baptized, and on the pastoral ministry of bishops.[4]

While it may be true, as Fr. Hussey suggests, that a renewed theology of the priesthood needs to be developed, our present theology of the Church as *communio* allows for a simultaneous expression of sacramental equality and hierarchical order and for a complementarity between the role of the priest and the role of the laity.[5] Lay ministers cannot replace the ordained, and the ordained do not make the ministry of the laity irrelevant. Both share in the Lord's vineyard.

Archbishop William Borders of Baltimore captured this insight with clarity and wisdom in his pastoral letter *You Are a Royal Priesthood*:

> The ordained ministry does not exist by or for itself, but only in and for the church. It exists to offer the service of leadership and sacramental nourishment through which it acts as a catalyst to enable and empower the whole community of the church to realize its mission in the world. Thus the theology of holy orders arises out of the theology of the church and not vice versa, and the apostolic responsibility inherent in the sacrament of orders does not stand apart from the responsibility and mission given to the entire priestly people of God. Those who are called to the ordained ministry fulfill their role through the service

of leading God's people in the fourfold ministry of the church—in proclaiming the Gospel, in worshiping, in building community and in offering healing service to human needs.[6]

The priesthood, in other words, only makes sense if there is a community to be served. For the priest exists for the sake of the people, not the people for the sake of the priest. This is not to suggest that the priest is merely an employee of the people, to be ordered about as they see fit. No, the priest is called and sent by God, vested with the power and responsibility of the ordained to act in the person of Christ. He is nonetheless there for the people, as his "ministerial priesthood is at the service of the common priesthood" of the faithful and directed to the "unfolding of the baptismal grace of all Christians."[7]

It should be underscored, however, that an essential difference exists between the common priesthood of the faithful and the ministerial, or hierarchical, priesthood. This essential difference "is not found in the priesthood of Christ, which remains forever one and indivisible, nor in the sanctity to which all of the faithful are called."[8] Rather, this essential difference exists because the ministerial priesthood is rooted in apostolic succession vested with sacred power consisting of the faculty and the responsibility of acting in the person of Christ the Head and Shepherd.[9]

It seems that what God has in mind at this juncture in salvation history is a deepening and broadening awareness about the nature of the Church as a community of collaborative ministry and about the authentic nature of priestly service.

One of the concerns raised by the development of lay ministry over the past thirty years is the temptation to clericalize the laity and to laicize the clergy.

First, there seems to be a growing perception that the lay person's faith is validated to the extent that he or she performs formal ministry within the Church or exercises a visible liturgical role. Certainly, as already noted, the laity's role in the liturgy has expanded tremendously, through service as lectors, eucharistic ministers, cantors, musicians, and those responsible for preparing people for Baptism and Matrimony.

Also the number of persons serving as full- or part-time lay ecclesial ministers in our parishes, diocesan offices, and church agencies has grown astronomically. For example, a national research study conducted by Msgr. Philip J. Murnion and David Delambo of the National Pastoral Life Center reveals that the number of lay persons (including vowed religious) working full- or part-time in formal parish ministry has grown 35 percent over the past seven years. The study also showed that 63 percent of all parishes now employ lay ministers. It further estimates that at least 3,500 laity can be found ministering in hospitals, health care institutions, prisons, seaports, and airports.[10] This explosion of formal lay ministries has been accompanied by a corresponding growth in graduate and certificate programs in ministry, diocesan-sponsored lay ministry programs, and national ministerial associations.

This growth of ecclesial ministries is a sign of health and vitality in the life of the Church. In *Ecclesia in America* (*The Church in America*), Pope John Paul II reiterates that "the renewal of the Church in America will not be possible without the active presence of the laity. Therefore, they are largely responsible for the future of the Church."[11] As promising and needed as these ministries are, however, it should never be communicated explicitly or implicitly that it is only through the exercise of these formal lay ministries or liturgical roles that the laity fulfill their baptismal call to holiness and ministry.

It is also critically important that we maintain the distinction between those ecclesial ministries that are entrusted to the laity appropriately because of their baptismal call (e.g., teacher, cate-chist, lector, parish council member) and those ministries, ordinar-ily reserved to the ordained, that are delegated to the laity by exception in case of need (e.g., parish administrator, parish life coordinator). As the interdicasterial document *Instruction on Certain Questions Regarding the Collaboration of the Non-Ordained Faithful in the Sacred Ministry of Priests* points out, this distinction should be recognized in the titles, rituals, and canonical and liturgical forms used for the designation and installation of such ministers.[12]

The key to an appropriate balance and harmonization between the roles of the ordained and the laity, I believe, lies in the leadership skills of collaboration wherein the priest is seen neither by himself nor with others as the sole minister in the Church but instead as the catalyst, facilitator, animator, motivator, and enabler who works with the laity to explore the interrelationships between the gifts and ministries within the Christian community and to facili-tate the development of such.

The 1976 U.S. bishops' document *As One Who Serves* captures well this catalytic role of the priest vis-à-vis the laity when the bish-ops compare the priest to an orchestra leader seeking to translate the vision of the composer into a harmonious blend of sound com-ing from a variety of instruments, many of which he cannot play himself.[13]

The truly effective priest for the twenty-first century, then, will be the one who sees himself as called not so much to deliver service but to empower others. He must assist the birth of the Church of the new millennium by giving witness to and bringing to fruition the Scriptures' vision of and the Second Vatican Council's exhortation to collegiality, collaboration, and shared responsibility, leading to a communal building-up of the Kingdom through the full utilization of each person's gifts.

In this latter regard, I believe the whole question of the role of women in the Church needs the special attention of the priest. It is easy to draw the line quickly at women's ordination and unbridled feminism. But there is a lot of leeway in between. Women are assuming roles and responsibilities in the Church, roles that they have never had before. Over 80 percent of those ministering in the Church on a full-time basis are women.[14] But, unfortunately, more women are also leaving the Church or are becoming alienated and frustrated. Women are experiencing the glass ceiling in new and more subtle ways. I don't know what the solution is, but I do believe—as the 1994 bishops' statement *Strengthening the Bonds of Peace: A Pastoral Reflection on Women in the Church and in Society* urges—that priests must actively recognize that the question of women's place in the Church is not solved and won't be resolved easily. Rather, the issue needs to be addressed on many levels and by many levels of church membership with openness to those who are seeking to make a positive contribution to the question on all points of the ideological spectrum.[15]

Priests are called to be ever conscious of the issue, ever sensitive to address hurts and slights, and ever willing to affirm women and their dignity and to provide opportunities for women to exercise positions of leadership and decision making in the Church. They must make the inclusion of others, and in particular of women, an integral part of their role as leaders in the Church.

Another challenge that demands immediate attention is the tendency (at least subconscious) to relegate those laity who do not exercise formal ministry or liturgical roles within the Church to second-class status or to the status of persons having a lesser call among the People of God. Historically we have shown this tendency with the distinction between the clergy and religious on the one hand, and the laity on the other, imagining the former as the doers and actors in the Church, and looking upon ordination and religious profession as elevating persons to a status of spiritual superiority. When this has happened, the laity in turn have been viewed as exercising a more modest, more passive role in the church community, helping out on kind of a temporary, standby basis when the father, brother, sister, or deacon needs assistance in fulfilling those roles that are essentially theirs—and in no way competing with those clergy and religious in holiness, prayerfulness, and spirituality.

It is essential, then, that those exercising lay ecclesial ministry or liturgical roles in the Church not be defined or presented as having a better or more noble role than other laity who do not exercise ministries geared to serving the faith community as such.

Akin to this concern is the tendency we have had since the Second Vatican Council to focus on the development of lay ecclesial ministries and liturgical roles almost to the detriment or exclusion of the laity's primary call to transform the world. This pitfall was cited in *Christifideles Laici*: "The Synod has pointed out that the post-conciliar path of the lay faithful has not been without its difficulties and dangers. In particular . . . [they experience] the temptation of being so strongly interested in Church services and tasks that some fail to become actively engaged in the responsibilities in the professional, social, cultural and political world."[16]

This issue was addressed strongly and clearly by the U.S. bishops in their pastoral statement *Called and Gifted: The American Catholic Laity*. In the section "Christian Service Ministry in the World," the bishops speak first about the laity's role and responsibility to bring Christian values and practices to bear upon "complex questions such as those of business ethics, political choice, economic security, quality of life, [and] cultural development" and to be an "extension of the Church's redeeming presence in the world."[17] It is only after they affirm the laity's normative secular ministry that the bishops speak about the call of the laity to ecclesial or church ministry. Hence, *Called and Gifted* offers an inclusive view of lay ministry in which the laity's church service is affirmed as ministry but wherein their service to family, work, and the world is held to be their primary and preeminent ministry.

Indeed, in an address on the vocations of the laity, entitled "Linking Church and World," delivered to the National Conference of Catholic Bishops at Collegeville, Minn., in June 1986, Bishop Raymond Lucker pointed out that "we have reversed [the] order. We have tended to call [lay] people first to ministries within the church community and secondarily (or at least with far less emphasis) to ministries for the transformation of society."[18]

It is important, therefore, that we correct this imbalance but not discourage or downplay in any way the creative new Church or the ecclesial ministries that have emerged; these have been vitally enriching and must continue to flourish and expand. We must give equal attention, however, to supporting and encouraging lay people in their ministries to the world; in the marketplace; in the areas of work, family, and leisure; and in all their ministries for the transformation of society. It is especially in the family and society, in marriage and work, in human sexuality, and in economics that this transformation takes place.

Consequently, it is a task of the Church to help the laity appreciate the call they have in the home, on the job, and in the neighborhood or community: a call to transform society and to make the message of the Gospel real in the family, social life, business transactions, and world of politics.

Furthermore, the Church must help its members make the connection between faith and work, between weekend liturgy and weekday responsibilities, and between seeing God's presence at the altar and at the desk, the sink, the farm, the labor union hall, the P.T.A. meeting, the political caucus, and the legislative chamber.

In the past, we encouraged, or seemed to have encouraged, lay people to find holiness by leaving the world instead of finding holiness in the world. Now we must recapture and develop practical ways to foster that sterling insight of the Council that the laity's unique role is to make Christ present in society and to transform political, economic, and social institutions in light of the Gospel.[19]

How can the priest help strike this important balance? Let me offer three concrete suggestions.

1. Priests must be more intentional in fostering lay spirituality. There is a widespread recognition that spirituality for the lay person should integrate work, civic obligations, political responsibilities, neighborhood activities, family life, education, and culture. Most lay persons, however, express frustration in seeking to effect this integration in their daily lives. Often they lament that the homilies they hear, the programs the Church offers, and the role models it provides do not speak to their daily struggles, or do not help them experience the Lord in their marriage commitments, interpersonal relations, family lives, and workplace relationships. They are seeking help in developing a practical spirituality that helps them to live their faith in a culture and society that offer little support.

Priests can give assistance in developing such a spirituality by interacting with laity in preparing homilies, listening to stories of the laity, tapping their visions, gleaning their insights, and treasuring their gifts. The future of ministry, then, must be shared not only in terms of roles and responsibilities but also in terms of receiving from the laity insights drawn from their lived experiences as to how the Scriptures and the teaching of our Church connect with everyday life.

Fostering spirituality for the laity will mean making available quality spiritual direction and counsel and providing opportunities for prayer, retreats, and spiritual renewal. The priority that the priest places on his own spiritual life will be helpful in making this a priority for the lay person as well. Priests who make spirituality a personal priority will also be inclined to foster small faith-sharing groups to help lay persons live out their family, work, and civic responsibilities from a spiritual core.

2. Priests must put into practice *Our Hearts Were Burning Within Us*, the document on adult faith formation that was approved by the U.S. bishops in November 1999, by making adult faith formation a priority and by helping lay people gain the resources needed for lifelong faith formation. This may mean that the parish underwrite the cost for businesspersons, scientists, officeholders, and others to attend workshops and conferences. It might entail theology courses regularly offered at times, places, and costs convenient for the laity. It may also mean, in many instances, hiring a competent staff person to attend imaginatively to this critical area in the life of the whole community.[20]

3. The priest must consciously focus on the laity's mission to the world. Through his preaching, teaching, and spiritual formation, he must foster a spirit of outward mission and seek to offer ways in which this can find concrete expression. Organizationally this might look like a network of small groups within a parish that are compassionately engaged with whatever segment of human need toward which God directs

them. Grounded in prayer and study, the laity can be motivated to act together as a gathered Church, or individually, as members "on mission" (for example, tutoring or visiting the homebound). The role of the priest is to keep before the groups and the people as a whole the gospel vision of our need to ally ourselves with the poor and the powerless. Without this kind of priestly leadership, small communities could become narcissistic enclaves, meeting to shield one another from the challenge of change.

In conclusion, let me suggest that the challenge of developing a meaningful relationship between priest and laity lies in balancing two fundamental principles that coexist in our post-Vatican II Church. On the one hand, the Second Vatican Council emphasizes the common dignity and equality that exists among all the members of God's people. All, therefore, are called to the same holiness of life, and all are entitled to become engaged actively in exercising the Church's mission to the world. On the other hand, the Council also highlights the hierarchical nature of the Church. We live as believers within a Church that has an appointed structure with predetermined ranks of authority.

These two notions—so evident in the conciliar documents and in the revised *Code of Canon Law*—are not contradictory, but they do create tension when it comes to such practical questions as how decisions get made in the Church, or to whom and how one is accountable. This tension is real at the level of the universal Church, and it also affects our local churches and our parish communities.

For the immediate future, then, we are faced with the challenge of living with this tension, with these two differing notions. One side stresses our fundamental equality as members of the Body of Christ; the other side stresses the structure and organization that the Body must have if we are to remain one in Christ. One side acknowledges the gifts of God that exist within individual believers; the other side stresses the diversity of functions and roles that must be lived out within the Christian community. Somewhere in between, we are expected to govern and to be governed, to minister and to be ministered to. The challenge, then, is to recognize the authority of those who hold pastoral office within the Church without diminishing the value of those laity who recognize their call to share leadership responsibility arising from Baptism, Confirmation, and the Eucharist.

The style of interaction between priests and laity must, therefore, be seen within the context of this creative tension. It must flow from an understanding of the fact that we are one family of the baptized and that it is the exercise of the collaborative priesthood of the baptized that most fully continues the sacramental presence of Christ in the world.

This understanding demands an interdependence and partnership between priests and laity. Priests have a serious responsibility to help all the members of the Church to discover, to develop, and to use their God-given gifts, talents, and charisms for the well-being of our Church and society. The laity have an equally serious responsibility to rediscover the scriptural revelation about the priesthood of all the faithful and the common vocation to holiness and ministry that they possess by virtue of Baptism. Such an understanding of Church, therefore, emphasizes that the Church is not a stratified or a clerically dominated society but a community of persons, all sharing in the priesthood of Jesus Christ and all called equally to be the People of God.

Such an understanding stresses, furthermore, that the Church is a community of collaborative ministry: a community in which each member is challenged to see his or her Baptism as a call to holiness and ministry; a community that seeks to help its members to discern the personal charisms given to them by the Spirit and to enable them to employ their gifts in the mission of the Church; a community whose ordained, vowed, and lay ecclesial ministers see the fostering of greater participation in the work of the Church and the building up of the kingdom as essential to their responsibility as leaders.

This understanding of ministry does not negate the unique and distinctive role of the ordained minister, the evangelical charism of the vowed, or the sterling gifts of the laity; but it underscores, as Archbishop William Borders points out so well in his pastoral letter *You Are a Royal Priesthood*, that "before any distinction of roles or offices in the church, we stand as one family of the baptized. It is the community as a whole to whom is given the primary responsibility for the mission of the church, and it is the whole community which stands as the first minister of the kingdom."[21]

NOTES

1   Second Vatican Council, *Lumen Gentium* (LG) (*Dogmatic Constitution on the Church*), no. 31. In Walter M. Abbott, ed., *The Documents of Vatican II* (New York: Crossroad, 1966).

2   National Conference of Catholic Bishops, *Called and Gifted for the Third Millennium* (Washington, D.C.: United States Catholic Conference, 1995), p. 15. Cf. John Paul II, *Christifideles Laici* (CL) (*The Vocation and the Mission of the Lay Faithful in the Church and in the World*) (Washington, D.C.: United States Catholic Conference, 1988), no. 20.

3   LG, no. 33.

4   M. Edmund Hussey, "Needed: A Theology of Priesthood," *Origins* 17:34 (February 4, 1988): 581.

5   Cf. Extraordinary Synod of Bishops, "The Final Report of the 1985 Extraordinary Synod of Bishops," *Origins* 15:27 (December 19, 1985): 448.

6   William Borders, "You Are a Royal Priesthood," *Origins* 18:11 (August 18, 1988): 177.

7   *Catechism of the Catholic Church*, 2nd ed. (Washington, D.C.: United States Catholic Conference, 2000), no. 1547.

8   Congregation for the Doctrine of the Faith, *Instruction on Certain Questions Regarding the Collaboration of the Non-Ordained Faithful in the Sacred Ministry of Priests* (Washington, D.C.: United States Catholic Conference, 1998), p. 6.

9   Cf. John Paul II, *Pastores Dabo Vobis* (*I Will Give You Shepherds*) (Washington, D.C.: United States Catholic Conference, 1992), no. 16.

10 Philip J. Murnion and David Delambo, *Parishes and Parish Ministers: A Study of Parish Lay Ministry* (New York: National Pastoral Life Center, 1999), passim. Cf. also Philip J. Murnion, et al., *New Parish Ministers: Laity and Religious on Parish Staffs* (New York: National Pastoral Life Center, 1992); Subcommittee on Lay Ministry, National Conference of Catholic Bishops, *Lay Ecclesial Ministry: The State of the Questions* (Washington, D.C.: United States Catholic Conference, 1999).

11 John Paul II, *Ecclesia in America* (*The Church in America*) (Washington, D.C.: United States Catholic Conference, 1999), no. 44.

12 Cf. *Instruction on Certain Questions*, op. cit.

13 Cf. Bishops' Committee on Priestly Life and Ministry, National Conference of Catholic Bishops, *As One Who Serves: Reflections on the Pastoral Ministry of Priests in the United States* (Washington, D.C.: United States Catholic Conference, 1977), p. 46.

14 Philip Murnion, et al., *New Parish Ministers*, op. cit., p. 27.

15 Cf. National Conference of Catholic Bishops, *Strengthening the Bonds of Peace: A Pastoral Reflection on Women in the Church and in Society* (Washington, D.C.: United States Catholic Conference, 1994).

16 CL, no. 2.

17 National Conference of Catholic Bishops, *Called and Gifted: The American Catholic Laity* (Washington, D.C.: United States Catholic Conference, 1980), p. 6.

18 Raymond Lucker, "Linking Church and World," *Origins* 16:7 (July 3, 1986): 150.

19 Cf. LG, no. 31.

20 Cf. National Conference of Catholic Bishops, *Our Hearts Were Burning Within Us: A Pastoral Plan for Adult Faith Formation in the United States* (Washington, D.C.: United States Catholic Conference, 1999).

21 "You Are a Royal Priesthood," op. cit., p. 170.

PRIESTHOOD IN
THE SERVICE OF JUSTICE

Most Reverend William S. Skylstad
Bishop of Spokane

Fr. Henri J. M. Nouwen in 1985 wrote *Love in a Fearful Land: A Guatemalan Story,*[1] an account of the ministry of Fr. Stan Rother, his love for the Mayan people, and his murder in Santiago Atitlan on July 28, 1981. Fr. Rother, a diocesan priest from the Archdiocese of Oklahoma City, had gone to Guatemala to serve the Mayans in the highlands on the shores of Lake Atitlan. Santiago Atitlan is one of several villages surrounding this beautiful volcanic lake.

Fr. Rother's death has become a powerful witness for the people whom he served. While his family chose to have him buried in Oklahoma, they permitted his heart and some of his blood to remain in a grave in Santiago Atitlan. That gravesite has become a place of prayer and reverence as parishioners continue to come and venerate his remembrance. A gravestone over the spot simply contains the words of Jesus: "There is no greater love than this: to lay down one's life for one's friends." Fr. Rother's love of people, his appreciation of the human dignity of every person, and his call for justice for the oppressed costed him his life. His martyrdom continues to stand as a source of great inspiration to us priests who labor in the vineyard of the Lord. We may not be asked to give our lives in martyrdom for the love of people, but his witness is a powerful reminder of our need to be faithful to God's call and God's people whom we serve.

One picks up a strong sense of fidelity in Fr. Rother's witness. Some months before his death, he returned home to Oklahoma because of danger to his life. His name was on a hit list. A strong compulsion in his heart led him back to the people whom he loved. He continued to serve them until the time of his murder. For us, too, God's call, the love of God's people, and the proclamation of the right ordering of relationships in society and in our world demand courage and fidelity.

I have visited Lake Atitlan several times since Fr. Rother's death in 1981. For almost forty years the Diocese of Spokane has had a special relationship with the Diocese of Solola as we have helped serve the local church there. Several times I have looked across the lake from the town of Panajachel to Santiago Atitlan and felt a profound sense of appreciation and gratitude. Even from a few kilometers away, a special place of witness becomes a source of prayerful gratitude and appreciation.

New Opportunities

Fr. Rother's witness has been multiplied many times over in countless stories of those who have courageously and faithfully labored in service to God's people and expressed to them the love of Jesus and of the Church. We priests occupy unusual positions as pastors and servants of the Gospel, positions that enable us to make a difference in society and in the human condition. Jesus' words in the beginning of the Gospel of Mark, "Repent and believe in the Good News" (1:15), remind us not only of the need for the conversion of our own hearts as ministers but the constant opportunities we have to facilitate the transformation of human hearts into a more just society.

We priests are present in almost every part of the world. There are few if any vocations in life that can so significantly impact people's lives and affirm the dignity of the human person. Francis Cardinal George, OMI, of Chicago once noted that the Church has gone to the ends of the earth. Now perhaps even the greater challenge is to go to the ends of people's hearts. The just word of God and the teaching of the Church can be and are a powerful leaven in the human family. The priest has an unusual opportunity to make justice come alive in people's hearts and lives.

In many ways the moment has never been more opportune nor more urgent to proclaim justice, respect for human life, and solidarity with the human family. The recent U.S. bishops' administrative board's statement *Faithful Citizenship: Civic Responsibility for a New Millennium* lists some of the signs of the times and challenges that face us:[2] in many of our cities in the United States a majority of our children never see the light of day in birth; indeed, 1.4 million children "are destroyed before birth every year." Twenty-five percent of our preschool children are growing up in poverty, in a nation in which the stock market continues to rise and wealth continues to accumulate. Some of our schools have "become almost war zones," and we are shocked by violence of parents towards their children and of youth who find a certain kind of glee in killing and violence. Hatred and intolerance continue to plague our nation; and here in the northwest, we find ourselves dealing with the headquarters of the Aryan Nation, a neo-Nazi group. (Recently, I saw a map of the locations of the headquarters of hate groups throughout the United States. Frankly, I was dumbfounded at how many swastikas were on the map all over the country.) Finally, we have a growing economy, but the gap between the rich and the poor continues to widen. More of our people are falling through the cracks.

OPEN OUR EYES

Families continue to be significantly impacted by poverty, which almost always leads to a lack of basic health care, inadequate housing, or even the loss of an entire way of life, such as we see with the American family farmer. Sensationalism, scandal in the highest echelons of government power, and uncivil political dialogue make for a tragic sign of misplaced values and dehumanizing lifestyles. The focus of political campaigns these days seems to be more upon who can raise the most money with the accompanying power that it gives, as contrasted to a message of political responsibility and genuine solidarity with people.

Violence has touched human hearts in our nation and around the world. Human life has become cheap and readily expendable in the continuum from abortion to escaping through drugs to ethnic and tribal cleansing.

We are called to community, to relationship. This call should give us a sense of urgency, eagerness, and enthusiasm for living and proclaiming the life-giving message of the Gospel. To paraphrase what G. K. Chesterton once said about "the Christian ideal," the Gospel hasn't failed—it's just not been tried yet. Dr. M. Scott Peck, in his recent book *A World Waiting to Be Born*, offers hopeful thoughts as we look to the future.[3] We should remind ourselves that we cannot rest on our laurels but must prophetically, courageously, and consistently address the need for building and strengthening relationships in the human community. According to the CIA's 1999 *World Factbook*, Rwanda's population is over 60 percent Catholic—how could disintegration of relationships in society and the respect for others collapse so quickly and tragically in the massive massacres? Recently I read an article by a priest from Rwanda, who lamented the fact that the Church never confronted in any significant way the deep tribal divisions there, even though on the surface the society seemed to be relatively calm. It took just the spark of a plane crash to initiate a human conflagration that still leaves us stunned.

We cannot procrastinate or delegate to someone else this work of proclaiming and sharing the powerful and transforming message of justice. In his book *The Kingdom of God*, Fr. John Fuellenbach, SVD, talks about Jesus coming to give us a vision of the kingdom.[4] St. Paul, in his letter to the Romans, reminds us of the kingdom of justice, peace, and joy. This vision of the kingdom should spark within us a sense of excitement and eagerness to share the Good News of Jesus.

CALL OF THE SPIRIT

That sense of vibrancy is beautifully captured in the words of Luke 4:18-19 as Jesus stands up in the synagogue in his home town of Nazareth and repeats the words of Isaiah 61:

> The spirit of the Lord is upon me,
>   because he has anointed me
>   to bring glad tidings to the poor.
> He has sent me to proclaim liberty to captives
>   and recovery of sight to the blind,
>   to let the oppressed go free
> and to proclaim a year acceptable to the Lord.

As St. Luke tells us, all in the synagogue had their eyes fixed on him. The moment was magnetic, powerful. Clearly Jesus' words had tremendous impact: as Jesus related his words to their hearts, they became angry and drove him out of town.

As the familiar saying goes, "one of the longest journeys in life is from the head to the heart." We should find our ministry of helping people to make that connection exciting and, of course, challenging. We are not in ministry only for the short term but for the long haul. Sometimes the journey from the head to the heart can be quick, wonderful, and affirming. But for most the trip is not that rapid. Constant reminders, continued proclamations, and movement of the Holy Spirit in our hearts make for years of gradual transformation. We must not lose heart, and we must not be intimidated by the enormity of the challenge that faces us. After all, you and I are mere instruments of the Lord. It is the Lord who will effect change of heart and transformation of lives.

Remarkable changes and technological development have had an impact on our world community. To be sure, there are many negative impacts from these developments; but even more importantly, we have seen our world community become, more and more, a global village. For us as presbyters in the Church, the opportunity has never been greater for helping to make a difference in the human heart and to make people's lives and the life of society all over the world more whole and more just.

VOICES OF THE MOMENT

We can appreciate several factors at the present moment that give us a springboard for our ministry of serving justice. First is a deepening appreciation of Sacred Scripture. Both the Old and New Testaments continue to provide us with a deepening awareness of the message of justice. The Old Testament prophets Jeremiah, Isaiah, Ezekiel, and Hosea are just a few examples of the powerful prophets of justice. The Advent readings remind us of the wonderful images of vision and hope. In Isaiah 11, the prophet shares his enthusiasm for what can be:

> Justice shall be the band around his waist,
> and faithfulness a belt upon his hips.
> Then the wolf shall be a guest of the lamb,
> and the leopard shall lie down with the kid;
> The calf and the young lion shall browse together,
> with a little child to guide them.
> The cow and bear shall be neighbors;
> together their young shall rest. . . . (5-7)

Some have said that the Second Vatican Council has helped the parable of the Good Samaritan to come alive in the Church. The story has tremendous application for our day. The poor fellow lying in the ditch symbolizes people all over the world who are hurting, who need our love, and whose rights need to be protected. The increased sensitivity to the needs and rights of our brothers and sisters is what justice does for the human family. The scene of the last judgment in Matthew 25 speaks powerfully to the foundation of our justice teaching. As Jesus shares in a very graphic way what our responsibilities are to one another, he emphatically connects us with every member of the human family: "Amen, I say to you, whatever you did for one of these least brothers of mine, you did for me" (40).

Several years ago I saw a documentary on the Discovery Channel about the Falkland war. Near the end of the documentary was an interview with a British soldier who talked about his experience of walking towards Stanley after a fierce firefight. He had passed by a badly injured young Argentinian soldier in the ditch along the side of the road. The young Argentinian in broken English cried out for help, but as the British soldier in the documentary explained, the Argentinian was the enemy and so the soldier had walked on. Suddenly the soldier burst into tears as he was being interviewed: "I know that Argentinian soldier in the ditch was a son of parents as I was. He probably also was a husband and father of children as I am. He was the enemy and so I walked on. I want to tell you war is hell" (my paraphrase). I don't know what moved this former soldier to appreciate in a whole new way that meeting on a snowy road as he marched towards Stanley. I can only presume that the Holy Spirit touched his heart in new appreciation and awareness. That's our exciting role as priests in the Church: to help people become aware of the power of God's word and the impact it has on our lives even in the most difficult moments. We have the wonderful mission of helping people to connect to God and to one another.

THE LEARNING CHURCH SPEAKS TO THE MOMENT

We have observed a tremendous development in the social teaching of the Church, a second development that aids us in proclaiming justice. Although we certainly find social concerns in the Church over the centuries, only recently has there been a tremendous development in that teaching, beginning with Pope Leo XIII's *Rerum Novarum*. The opening words of the *Gaudium et Spes* (*Pastoral Constitution on the Church in the Modern World*) of the Second Vatican Council were powerfully prophetic: "The joy and hope, the grief and anguish of the men of our time, especially of those who are poor or afflicted in any way, are the joy and hope, the grief and anguish of the followers of Christ as well."[5] One of the great legacies in the teaching of Pope John Paul II will certainly be his tremendous contribution to the body of social teaching of the Church through his encyclicals and apostolic letters. There are almost twenty of them! I am sure this legacy of his teaching will be a gift for centuries to come.

The pastoral letters and statements of bishops in the United States have provided a wonderful treasure for helping make the Gospel come alive in our teaching and preaching. Bishops around the world have issued pastoral letters concerning the conditions of their respective societies, helping people to connect the Gospel to their daily living and to political situations in which they find themselves.

A few years ago I had the opportunity of visiting the country of Malawi as a board member for Catholic Relief Services (CRS). Shortly after arriving in the country, CRS staff members made me aware of a relatively brief pastoral letter by the bishops of that country, "Living Our Faith," issued at the beginning of Lent in 1992. The bishops talked about dignity and unity of humankind, the aspiration to greater equality and unity, participation in all of public life, and a system of justice that works fairly. Almost immediately after the letter was issued, the bishops were thrown into prison, scheduled to be executed. If it hadn't been for the diplomatic community, their lives probably would not have been spared. Malawi's then president for life was extremely angry. New elections were called for, and he was voted out of office. I saw from a distance, too, the three luxurious residential palaces he built in a country that is one of the poorest in Africa. They were huge edifices.

While I was meeting with some parishioners in the city of Mzuzu in the northern part of Malawi, one of the ladies told me: "You can't believe how our country has changed. We still have problems, but things are so much better now. It's wonderful!" One of the sisters observed that everyone knows what a tremendous impact the bishops had made with their teaching. What a remarkable transformation was brought about in that society by the courage of those seven bishops!

Our Situation in the
Marketplace Speaks to the Moment

A third factor that aids our service of justice is that the Church's great sensitivity to human rights and advocacy for the poor, vulnerable, and disenfranchised has become more and more a part of our tradition. As *Faithful Citizenship* indicates, our Catholic Church brings three major assets to the marketplace: (1) our "consistent moral framework"; (2) our "everyday experience" as Church, as evidenced in our social outreach through organizations such as Catholic Charities, Catholic Relief Services, and the involvement of our parishes all over the land in social mission and outreach; and (3) our assets as a "community of citizens."[6] Our Catholic community is large and diverse in political makeup, in ethnic backgrounds, and in geographic presence, whether in an urban, suburban, or rural setting.[7] In addition, as the bishops describe in their 1999 statement *In All Things Charity*, the U.S. Catholic Church "sponsors the largest voluntary network of social services, health care, and education in the United States."[8]

Our Global Solidarity Speaks to the Moment

The reality of our increased connectedness as a Church is a fourth factor in our service of justice. For the first time in our history, we have truly become a Church universal. Mobility, communication, and the opportunity for interaction within the Church have never been greater. Such interconnectedness should move us beyond insularity and parochialism to a truer sense of our being Church all over the world and of the opportunity to be present in service and love to every person around the globe.

We hear much today about stewardship of time, talent, and treasure. The lived expression of stewardship is far more difficult than its proclamation. However, we priests have an unusual opportunity to share the powerful, life-giving message of the Gospel and the social teaching of the Church. We have the opportunities to be stewards of the moment and give witness to the gifts we have received individually and in the Body of Christ. We must not fail the moment or the people whom we serve. Over and above that, I personally find the opportunity to help change our world and people's lives to be an exciting opportunity in our ministry.

Some years ago, shortly before she died, I heard Sr. Thea Bowman, FSPA, speak at the bishops' summer meeting at Seton Hall in Newark, N.J. Her sense of enthusiasm couldn't help but leave its mark upon all who heard her. In a similar way, I have heard Helen Alvare of the Pro-Life Activities Office at the National Conference of Catholic Bishops speak movingly about respecting life. Her words were filled with a sense of excitement and enthusiasm that was truly contagious. Those qualities should also characterize our own service and proclamation as we go about the Lord's work as ministers of justice. I am reminded of Carlo Maria Cardinal Martini's comment in his book on communication that "joy is a mother of communication." We not only sing a joyful song but live a joyful life and message.

TEN SUGGESTIONS

I offer ten suggestions as to how we might go about forming the vision and meeting the challenge of bringing about a more just world:

1. *Holiness of Life.* If we are not profoundly connected to the Trinity in prayer, intimacy, and worship, then the message we preach rings shallow and hollow. Jesus' words in John 15:5, "I am the vine, you are the branches," should remind us constantly from where our life, vibrancy, and vision come. We are nourished by the Bread of Life

and encouraged by the Eucharist to be foot washers in a thousand and one ways. Our solidarity with one another should be a source of great affirmation and encouragement as we minister in faith. Constant and serious attention to growth in our spirituality is critical for us to be effective, loving priests in the Church. Continued conversion of heart should be our ongoing goal.

2. *Proclaimers of the Word.* The Word of God is rich and, as St. Paul reminds us in Hebrews 4:12, "sharper than any two-edged sword." Through our skill in preaching the word, we hopefully can provide the opportunity of the word to pierce the human heart and to transform the stony heart into a heart of flesh, as Ezekiel reminds us (cf. 11:19). Our attention to growing personally in the word must be a constant effort. Prayerful reflection on the Scriptures and careful attention to praying the liturgy of the hours each day are great opportunities for growing in the word. Our challenge is to make the word of God come alive within us and in the hearts of those whom we serve. None of us should accept that challenge lightly or casually.

3. *Presiders of Eucharist.* What a gift and privilege for us to be presiders of Eucharist! Especially at the celebration of Eucharist we help our people find Jesus in their lives through word, sacrament, and community. We also help them to appreciate that as they leave the church building they move into the world as a eucharistic people. They too are to become "foot washers of humanity." Jesus as the Bread of Life has called all of us to go forth: "As I have done for you, so you should also do" (Jn 13:15).

4. *Relationship with One Another.* As a Church universal, we have the continued responsibility of helping parishioners to appreciate how we are Church together and how we as part of God's kingdom are connected to the whole human family. In a powerful scene at the end of the movie *Schindler's List,* the industrialist Oscar

Schindler and his wife are about to take leave of the Jewish community as the Nazi war machine collapses. He and his wife are surrounded by the community he had saved by placing them on his list. He looks down at his lapel to see a relatively large Nazi emblem made of gold. He takes the emblem off of his lapel, holds it for a moment in his hand, and then looks to the group about him as he breaks down in tears, wondering how many more names and lives he could have "bought" for the list with the worth of the emblem. It was a remarkable moment of connection.

As proclaimers of the Gospel and the teaching of the Church, we have the opportunity to help our sisters and brothers connect their wallets, their checkbooks, and their investment portfolios to the human family. We are only temporary stewards of these gifts. There are remarkable examples in our Church and in our society of how people use these gifts and resources in a prophetically generous way.

5. *The Presbyterate.* We are all members of the presbyterate of a particular church or of a religious community of men. Our relationships with our bishops or religious superiors should not be weakened by ideology, personal likes or dislikes, or personalities. The temptation to give in to the distraction of a lesser value compared to our unity as a presbyterate or a community of religious men can be considerable. We as a presbyterate are in union with our bishop not because he may have many gifts, possess a very pleasing personality, or (hopefully) provide a great witness, but because he is our bishop. Although more recently we have placed a lot more emphasis on the need for fraternity in our presbyterates and religious communities, even more importantly we must witness to our unity with one another, given all of our warts and moles, our limitations, or our brokenness and failings. A football team doesn't do well if there is disunity on the team. We don't do well in Church either if we allow our respect, reverence, and solidarity with one another in the universal Church to be weakened in any way. Like a married couple who must

base their love for one another on a decision rather than romantic attraction, we too must constantly say "yes" to our presbyterate, to our bishop, to our Holy Father, and to the Church universal.

6. *The Culture of Life.* Pope John Paul II, in his recent encyclical *Evangelium Vitae* (*The Gospel of Life*), powerfully encourages us to advance the culture of life in our world.[9] Our task as preachers of the Gospel is to help ourselves and others see insightfully the real devastation and dehumanization that occur through the "culture of death." The signs of the devastating consequences of the culture of death are all about us. We priests are to be promoters of life—and of the more abundant life that Jesus has promised us.

7. *Simplicity of Lifestyle.* We are called to live a simple lifestyle and identify with the *anawim*. The poorest of the poor are our brothers and sisters; and as Archbishop James Lyke, OFM, the former archbishop of Atlanta, used to say, "We are evangelized by the poor." Let's face it—we priests are well taken care of, and we have security like no one else in our society. We need to be grateful and as generous as we can be with our gifts and our resources. The way we play, dine, vacation, and otherwise use our resources point to our lifestyle. We also need to connect to our checkbook and our Visa card to see how they relate to our poorer brothers and sisters.

8. *Proclamation of Justice.* The proclamation of justice is a constitutive element of our priestly ministry. I hope we are past the day when a particular priest, engaged significantly in the social ministry and teaching of the Church, is considered to be on the left, or far left. To be sure, every priest has specific gifts. Every priest is gifted in one part of ministry perhaps more than another. But clearly together we are in the ministry of addressing issues like respect for life, racism, welfare reform, health care reform, gender equality, ethnic diversity in our Church, violence, the plight of the migrant, and oppression.

9. *Solidarity with the Human Family.* We are signs of unity to people who see us. We live out that unity through action and focus in our ministry. *Called to Global Solidarity,* a statement by the U.S. bishops on the international challenges for U.S. parishes, reminds us of our relationship with the world community.[10] Visits, relationships, sister parishes, or sister dioceses are expressions of our lived-out solidarity with the Church and with the human family. My life was forever changed after spending six years on the board for Catholic Relief Services. During that time I had the good fortune of a two-week visit each year: three times to countries in Central America, once to South America, and twice to Africa. Each time I came home humbled and grateful. On each trip I took about 150 photos. Periodically I take out one of the groups of photos and look through them. It's almost like a little retreat experience. How relationships in God's family nourish and transform us!

10. *A Joyful Hope.* We are priests of the kingdom, and we strive to live prophetically a vision for the kingdom that's here and to come. In our ministry we are in the business of living vibrantly a joyful hope. We are hopeful not because we see a light at the end of the tunnel, but as St. Paul reminds us because we hope in Divine Providence because the Lord is with us and the Holy Spirit will guide us and teach us. We strive to be humble instruments of the Lord, never knowing how we might be the planters of seeds or tillers of the ground of life. After all, it is the Lord who gives the increase and who ultimately makes "all things work [together] for good for those who love God, who are called according to his purpose" (Rom 8:28).

As we begin the new millennium, we priests enter a new age of opportunity, proclamation and witness. The Lord can use us as his servants—as prophets of justice, as bearers of the word in our hearts and in our ministry, as priests united with one another and our Church—to proclaim justice to the world and to bring about a continuing right ordering of relationships. The time has never been more right or opportune. Let us go forth!

NOTES

1   Cf. Henri J. M. Nouwen, *Love in a Fearful Land: A Guatemalan Story* (Notre Dame, Ind.: Ave Maria Press, 1985).

2   Administrative Board, National Conference of Catholic Bishops, *Faithful Citizenship: Civic Responsibility for a New Millennium* (Washington, D.C.: United States Catholic Conference, 1999), p. 2.

3   Cf. M. Scott Peck, *A World Waiting to Be Born* (New York: Bantam Books, 1993).

4   Cf. John Fuellenbach, *The Kingdom of God: The Message of Jesus Today* (Techny, Ill.: Divine Word Publications, 1989).

5   Second Vatican Council, *Gaudium et Spes* (*Pastoral Constitution on the Church in the Moden World*), no. 1. In Austin Flannery, ed., *Vatican Council II: The Conciliar and Post Conciliar Documents*, new rev. ed. (Northport, N.Y.: Costello Publishing Company, 1996).

6   *Faithful Citizenship*, pp. 10-11.

7   Ibid., p. 11.

8   National Conference of Catholic Bishops, *In All Things Charity: A Pastoral Challenge for the New Millennium* (Washington, D.C.: United States Catholic Conference, 1999), p. 8.

9   Cf. John Paul II, *Evangelium Vitae* (*The Gospel of Life*) (Washington, D.C.: United States Catholic Conference, 1995).

10 Cf. National Conference of Catholic Bishops, *Called to Global Solidarity: International Challenges for U.S. Parishes* (Washington, D.C.: United States Catholic Conference, 1998).

Priesthood in the Midst of Cultural Diversity

Most Reverend Gerald R. Barnes
Bishop of San Bernardino

In the early 1960s, Pulitzer Prize-winning novelist Edwin O'Connor wrote a novel called *The Edge of Sadness*. It is the story of a priest and an Irish family in Boston in the 1960s as it portrays the end of an era and the beginning of a new journey in life. The main character is Father Kennedy, an Irish priest and recovering alcoholic, who silently and sadly watches the end of the Irish ghetto and the influx of the new immigrants, the new faithful. The following is a passage from the book that speaks of the world and parish itself in transition.

> Saint Paul's: what a strange parish it is, really. Days, even weeks go by, and I don't even think of this; then, without preparation of any kind, there comes a moment—such as this one, at the beginning of a glorious day—when suddenly all the lights seem to be turned on at once, piercing the comfortable protection of routine, and I am confronted with the cold fact of Saint Paul's. It is called Old Saint Paul's, but there is no New Saint Paul's—the adjective refers only to the age of the parish. The church itself is the perfect mirror of the district: once, three generations ago,

active, prosperous, in a way even noble; today, a derelict, full of dust and flaking paint and muttering, homeless, vague-eyed men. This section of the city is dying and so is Old Saint Paul's. In a sense it is hardly a parish at all any more, but a kind of spiritual waterhole: a halting place for transients in despair. Still, we have our permanent families, those who live and stay here: Syrians, Greeks, some Italians, a few Chinese, the advance guard of the Puerto Ricans—a racial spectrum whose pastor I am. Here the pastor cuts quite a different figure than he does in one of the old, compact, all-Irish parishes. I know those parishes well. I was raised in one; I have in fact been pastor of one. Now I am here—and it should be said that this is hardly regarded as a promotion. Yet I have no complaints, not a single one, for this parish has come to mean something so special to me that I can't begin to say or explain. . .

Well, my point is that in those other parishes there does exist, invariably, this peculiar rapport between the priest and the people, and I suppose it springs largely from their knowledge that he is one of them—that he is from their own particular branch of the tree. The result is that whether they love him or fear him or respect him or admire him or distrust him, they are aware of him, he does enter their daily lives, he is a part of them.

In Old Saint Paul's, not so. These people are good people—at least I think they are: after almost a year here, I know them scarcely at all. I say Mass for them (and they come: in fair numbers on a Sunday, very few if any on a weekday); I hear their confessions (despite certain obvious difficulties, for I am no linguist); sometimes I baptize them, marry them, bury them; occasionally I go to their homes on sick calls. There are the formal, necessary points of contact between the shepherd and his flock—beyond them we do not go. They accept me as their priest, but after that they keep their distance—and I must admit (and this is perhaps my fault, my dereliction) that I keep mine. And I must admit this too: that sometimes, in the rectory, at night, I think with a little longing of the old days and the old ways—because, after all, a man may turn his back on something and still remember it. . . .[1]

O'Connor captures in a few simple words the feeling that comes as we watch the world that we have known so well become something very different. How often we have gathered together in priestly assemblies and longed for the old days when authority was clear and we lived in a world of one dominant and discernable culture. How often we have moaned silently to ourselves at the complexity of a multicultural and multi-dramatic liturgical celebration. I will endeavor in this essay to view some of the root causes of our difficulties in multicultural ministry. I will also utilize a model from the world of secular spirituality in order to find another road to sharing the message of Christ with all of our sisters and brothers.

The question arises of whether we can, as John Paul II calls us to do, proclaim with joy and conviction a message of the Church in America, and speak of Jesus Christ, the human face of God and the divine face of man? It is this proclamation that truly makes an impact on people, awakens and transforms hearts—in a word, converts. However, the old philosophical axiom of "I cannot give what I do not have" is often heard among us. How can I proclaim a message I do not have? In asking this question, we are like Father Kennedy, the priest in *The Edge of Sadness*: seeking to serve but failing to connect.

Perhaps we, like Father Kennedy, need to view our own past in order to gain a sense of our own present. John Paul II writes often of our great diversity, the stresses of that diversity, and the need to be one Church. So let us begin by examining some of our formational roots.

We come from a variety of formational models. For many of us, our experiences ranged from the strict rigorism and discipline of the '40s and '50s to the spirit of *aggiornamento* of the '60s. Let us, however, look with attention to the formational programs of the 1970s and 1980s, which in many respects were our first efforts at connecting with this new face of Jesus that we now encounter in our changing church.

In the 1970s and 1980s there grew a desire to form priests who were more culturally aware. Ethnic diversity became a new concern because our candidates were now coming from new places. Members of ethnically-centered communities now became desired as candidates. Yet simply to recruit was not enough—we needed to retain those whom we had recruited. Many studies of seminary programs told us that we needed to form priests who were secure both in their own identities and in the worlds that they were about to serve. The notion of a new kind of missionary was being born. This new missionary must now serve in the missions of his own neighborhood. The new missionary must be one who, like the missionaries of old, can embody the Gospel in its fullest sense. This requires one who understands the language, the culture, and the dreams of the people that he serves. This, of course, means that in order to prepare one to serve in these new missions—missions that are very much alive in our own country—we must do more than have seminarians eat tacos on the Feast of Our Lady of Guadalupe or eat egg rolls on the Lunar New Year. We began to realize that we must be open to being receivers of the word of God as well as the proclaimers. And we cannot settle for mere superficial modes of cultural connection.

We began in the 1970s and 1980s to view the cultural mix from which our seminaries had sprung. Previously we had believed that we had a "universal program," one-size-fits-all, that enabled us to form anyone into a good priest if he would only learn English and adapt to our world and our spirituality. This assumption proved not to be valid. We also worked on the long-held notion that we had only to fine-tune our existing efforts for them to work. And perhaps our last, greatest error came from assuming that our programs of formation did not in fact have any cultural bias or seeds of prejudice.

The idea that we could be all things to all people was for us a necessary foundation for our seminaries and eventually for our lives as priests. Now an interesting disparity also existed. As a U.S. Church we could accept the ethnic nature of religious communities whose foundations were clearly European, Latin, or Asian in origin. One would expect a certain ethnic flavor to exist in the mission house of the Divine Word missionaries or community house of Irish Christian Brothers. We knew there was always a hint of the old country.

However, we believed that our diocesan seminaries reflected our openly democratic society. We felt that we could include everyone in our seminary system, and our further conviction was that there were no elements of any cultural superiority that would exclude anyone. After all, are we not a nation that is truly a great melting pot? We have seen the results of our efforts to assimilate everyone into the parish as long as their ultimate goal is to look and speak and act like us.

To realize that it is not simply a matter of being a good American, but of being a good Christian, we need only remember the struggle of the early Church, as seen in Acts 15:6-12:

The apostles and the presbyters met together to see about this matter. After much debate had taken place, Peter got up and said to them, "My brothers, you are well aware that from the early days God made his choice among you that through my mouth the Gentiles would hear the word of the gospel and believe. And God, who knows the heart, bore witness by granting them the holy Spirit just as he did us. He made no distinction between us and them, for by faith he purified their hearts. Why, then, are you now putting God to the test by placing on the shoulders of the disciples a yoke that neither our ancestors nor we have been able to bear? On the contrary, we believe that we are saved through the grace of the Lord Jesus, in the same way as they." The whole assembly fell silent, and they listened while Paul and Barnabas described the signs and wonders God had worked among the Gentiles through them.

"FOR THERE IS NO JEW, OR GREEK, FREE OR SLAVE IN THE KINGDOM"

Perhaps we must begin by examining our own world with a critical but gentle heart. I would like to include one more example from the world of formation before we move on to our present reality. In the 1970s and 1980s efforts were made to create programs called "cross-cultural intensives." The cross-cultural intensive was designed to place predominantly "first-world" theological students in a living situation with "third-world poor" in such places as the streets of Gary, Ind., the barrios of San Antonio, Texas, or the multicultural mélange of South Central Los Angeles. In the 1970s places like Gary or the colonias of the Rio Grande Valley of Texas were riddled with great unemployment, violence, and soul-destroying poverty. The populations were predominantly

African American, Hispanic, and Asian. The one common factor that reached beyond culture was always poverty. Many were soon to discover that the world of the barrio, the ghetto, the segregated community was, figuratively speaking, another planet compared to the comforts of a Chicago suburb or a small town in Iowa. The students were to experience a "mission in reverse," and they were to live from the generosity and hospitality of the poor. They were simply inserted into the world of the other.

Of course, the results of this kind of radical training were varied. Some of the students were shell-shocked and totally appalled at what they saw. Others were lacerated with guilt at being part of the "white establishment," which was said to be the cause of this urban horror. Others made friends and learned about some of their own prejudices and the prejudices of those with whom they lived. They began to learn that every culture has value and has also a great need to be healed. It is true that Jesus walked with impunity, breaking cultural taboos as he sat with publicans and sinners. Jesus never ceased to be a Jew, nor did he cease to call his world to reform. Jesus healed all who came forth, but he called them "to change their lives." To put on the person of the Christ becomes the greatest cross-cultural leap of all.

Let us now, after our brief reflection on our past, look at our present. We return to our friend Father Kennedy of *The Edge of Sadness*. As the novel progresses, we learn that Father Kennedy has himself become one of the broken ones: we learn that he is an alcoholic. His "flaw" has placed him in a world outside the comfortable confines of respectable clergy. But in this exile he becomes able to connect with the very ones whom John Paul II calls us forth to evangelize, and into whose lives we are called to enter. The risky part, as Father Kennedy learns, is that the poor must now enter into his.

It is now the year 2000, and workshops abound with theories and thoughts about multicultural ministry. A whole new vocabulary has erupted that deals with a new reality in the Church. We speak now with a combination of theological openness and political correctness. In our efforts to become inclusive we can sometimes lose ourselves in a sea of words whose meanings become, in fact, meaningless. Pluriformity, diversity, culture, diversity of self, and so forth become so multi-interpretive that one is not sure out of which theology we speak, or even what planet we are coming from. We no longer have just a language barrier to overcome, but a meaning barrier as well.

For a moment I ask that we reflect on a secular institution that has managed to be successful in a pluriform society like our own, and on an international level as well: Alcoholics Anonymous (AA). AA is a group that effectively reaches across all cultural, social, and economic barriers. One can attend a meeting with individuals of every vocational and religious background. There is no prohibition nor is there any obstacle in entering the lives of the Other, and there is a real belief in "a power greater than ourselves" that can restore us to wholeness, sanity, and new life. In AA there is a strong element of service, which is punctuated by a real spirit of humility. Imagine an affluent lawyer emptying ashtrays and bringing coffee to a former convicted felon! AA is a program of attraction, not promotion. How does it work, and can it benefit us in our quest to minister in this brave new world we see before us?

The AA experience begins with the admission of common brokenness; that is, we are all flawed and we each carry within us the seeds of our own salvation and destruction. Dr. Ernest Kurtz calls it "The Spirituality of Imperfection." Every person, every aggregate of persons, and every culture is in some way flawed. Each one of us carries the remembrance of our own sin and redemption. In AA a kind of brutal honesty exists among its members, but coupled with that is the ability to share "our experience, strength, and hope" with each other—like Father Kennedy, who learned that it was only in accepting his fall from grace that he could, in humility, find his God and the God of those around him.

Not everyone needs to be a courageous saint like Matt Talbot to minister, but perhaps we need the humility of a Cure of Ars to do it effectively. Imagine a priest at Sunday Mass admitting that he does not have all the answers, and then giving evidence to those in the community by opening the doors of Christ—by unsealing his heart and even inviting strangers into his home. I am not suggesting public confession, but I am suggesting that the AA dictum of rigorous honesty and openness is possible. In the words of Martin Luther King Jr., "the truth will set us free." Can I admit that I am a recovering racist, a recovering egotist, a recovering sexist? Can I admit to others the tragic flaw that is a part of my own being? It is said that only when I allow the grace of God to heal my sinfulness can I truly reach out to my brothers and sisters and know that that same grace can heal them. Our new experience becomes the unbridled love of a God who will never let any of us go.

The second notion that can provide a useful comparison is the opportunity in an AA meeting for everyone to share their "faith and redemption" in terms that are real to them and to have the respectful attention of those around them. One can be either as grandiloquent as Sir John Gielgud or be as articulate as Sylvester Stallone—and still be heard.

I make this comparison because we so often view religious customs and practices a bit askance. Further, we find that we tend to view differences as insurmountable obstacles to faith and communication. But if we first see the areas of commonality, the brokenness we all possess, the hopes we all pray for, and the salvation we all seek—and then sit and try to merely hear with attention—a unity begins to form. In one of my local parishes, the pastor recounts how a group of Mexican immigrants and former Vietnamese boat-people found a common experience in the notion of exile. Each knew the pain of the loss of one's homeland; each knew discrimination; each cherished family, ancestors, and children. Each possessed a great love for the Blessed Mother. And despite the lack of a strong common language, they created a unifying bond.

The key was having a safe and respectful place to share God's word and their lives in their own way. The process was not unlike an AA meeting. The safe and respectful place that must be open to share God's word and sacraments must, of course, be our own churches. Yet the churches themselves must have signs of those who pray there and share there. There should be room for Our Lady of Guadalupe, Our Lady of Sorrows, and icons that reflect the soul of the people. In a church in our diocese where AA meetings are held daily, a copy of the Serenity Prayer in both English and Spanish is on the wall. Hope is for all without reserve.

As an aside, we too as priests must be willing to share with one another as brothers in Christ. We often fail to enter into the lives of those with whom we share ministry. We need only look at our ethnic diversity as clergy and realize that this must be our starting point toward simply being fellow pilgrims and companions. I once heard a somewhat officious and all-knowing clergyman state, "It is good that we have those Vietnamese priests, but when are we going to get some American vocations?" Our sensitive friend related this excellent commentary to a group of African American and Mexican American priests. Paul's words ring true: We must put on the person of Christ.

Finally, in AA there is an effort to strive for simplicity: "Keep it simple." Often in the Church we create impossible obstacles for the very people we seek to evangelize. Our concern for parish boundaries, the annulment system, and the very act of helping families in the process of religious education are but a few of the very complex U.S. legal notions that often repel, instead of attract, those whose experience of Church is so much different from ours. Imagine demanding a baptismal certificate from a family from San Salvador whose home parish and village is now nothing more than bloodied ground. Or asking a Vietnamese candidate for diaconate to enter into a formation program only after his *wife* is fluent in English. We must strive for a spirit of the law, not an unreal adherence to the letter.

My final reflection comes from John 4:4-42, with which we are all familiar: Jesus and the woman at the well. We see in this exchange the paradigm of cross-cultural ministry. The Samaritan woman's first response to Jesus was one of fear, resentment, and generations of suspicion. Jesus' first retort was one of invitation, but an invitation that was neither understood nor accepted. Jesus again offers and is again refused. But soon a common ground is reached: the common experience of thirst—thirst of a physical kind, and an even deeper thirst of the spiritual kind. We all thirst, we all hope for something more. It is, I believe, the common ground. Jesus, however, did not stop with merely pointing out the spiritual need he saw, and he accepted and challenged the woman despite her checkered past. He did not hold back from receiving her just because she did not possess an appropriate annulment form, or was a single mother, or came from a faith-journey different from his own. Jesus did not reject her for her different culture, one that had no love for Jesus' "background." Jesus accepted her and challenged her and was affected by her as he acknowledged who he was as Messiah.

John Paul II writes that "Jesus is the good news of salvation made known to people yesterday, today and forever." The simplicity of his manner and his choices must be a normative (i.e., model) for everyone in the work of evangelization. It is in these words—and in the humble examples of an Irish American novelist, a secular group of alcoholics, and those dedicated to formation—that I have endeavored to provide some thoughts for your consideration.

This question still arises: Is there a method or a plan that one can follow to minister effectively in a cross-cultural context? The answer, I feel, is ultimately a simple one. In our diocese on the West Coast, we have an older priest, a former Trappist, who is one of the senior members of our diocese. The priest, known as Fr. De, is Italian in background and is from the eastern part of the United States. Fr. De is known as a priest with whom everyone feels comfortable. He knows how to listen. He knows how to laugh. He knows how to share his faith. And he allows others to share theirs in their own ways. Fr. De is a friend to those in prison, to those who are poor, to those who do not know our language, to those who live in fear. Fr. De, as he is happy to tell you, is just another pilgrim in his way to find his God. And as De will always point out, one does not make a pilgrimage alone. It is in men like De that we find a model of where we should be.

I end with just one more example garnered from a Mexican grandmother: "There is always room at the table for one more. Never leave anyone at the door. Invite them in. Who knows, it may be Jesus himself."

NOTE

1   Edwin O'Connor, *The Edge of Sadness* (Boston: Little, Brown and Company, 1961), pp. 13-14.

THE PRIEST AS ADMINISTRATOR: REDISCOVERING OUR TRADITION OF PASTORAL LEADERSHIP

Reverend Blase J. Cupich
Bishop of Rapid City

A DAY IN THE LIFE OF FATHER JACK

The stack of messages tacked to the bulletin board begged for attention as Father Jack returned to the rectory from hospital visits. The afternoon must have been busy for Suzie, the parish secretary and a single mom of two very active teens. It had been a full but fulfilling day for Jack as well. He had anointed Florence and prayed with her family in the last days of a long but losing battle with cancer. Steve, rushed to the hospital last night with chest pains, had needed encouragement and calming from a trusting voice. Jack also briefly stopped to congratulate Teri, who after three miscarriages had just given birth to a healthy baby boy, Jeff Jr.

The note on top of the pile was a hard-to-read message from Irv: "Finished setting up your computer—you're now online. Your temp email name—FROSTY!" "Frosty" was Irv's whimsical reference to the previous weekend's homily, in which Jack made the mistake of revealing his boyhood nickname. Instead of alluding to those youthful blond locks, "Frosty" now could just as easily refer to his shiny pate—a humorous paradox not lost on the congregation.

While he had been at the hospital, Jennifer and Sam had called to schedule their second marriage prep appointment, noting that they hoped that they "passed the test." Adam, the stewardship committee chair, had also passed by the office with the list of presenters for next month's appeal. He wanted Father's approval and asked, "Could you visit with us soon to come up with a catchy theme that also fits the Scriptures of that weekend? The committee thinks we should make a push this year to go after the one-third of the parish who never donate."

Emily's mom had phoned to say that Emily had the flu and would not serve at Mass tonight. "Could you find a sub for her? Sorry, Father, I tried." Harriet and Allen's seventh-grade son, Jason, had been "tossed from class in school today. They called *demanding* a meeting ASAP with Father J, the principal, and the teacher." Could be sticky, he thought. Harriet had just won a seat on the parish school board. At the urging of other board members, who considered Allen a good donor prospect, Jack had encouraged her to run.

Frank, his old college roommate, had rung to invite him to "escape" after the holidays for a week of golf down at his winter home in Phoenix. He and his wife Ginger had retired four years before. Frank is financially comfortable after thirty years in the same job. Wearied by the workload of an executive, he had decided to "hang up his Daytimer."

And finally, the diocesan finance office had phoned *twice* to give a "gentle reminder" that the monthly financial report with midyear budget projections was due today. They also want to know if he remembered to re-register the parish tax ID number as required by the state treasurer for the new century. The chancellor had sent the forms out ten days ago. It was probably in the pile of unopened envelopes, one of many from diocesan offices that he just hadn't gotten to yet. He chuckled at the penitential plea that Pete, the neighboring pastor, coined in response to the ever-increasing deluge of missives from the chancery: "*Curia eleison!*"

With Mass scheduled in just over an hour, Jack decided to pray vespers, which was his habit before Mass. The messages could wait.

"In God alone is my soul at rest; my help comes from him . . ." the psalm began. The reading for Advent also struck him: "In the Lord's eyes, one day is as a thousand years, and a thousand years are as a day." Yes, but the days have changed over the nearly four decades since ordination. In the earlier years, parish life had fewer demands. Or was it that there had been more people to carry the workload? The sisters took the school, trained and scheduled the servers, and performed countless other tasks, for which he knows he and others never fully expressed appreciation. Councils and boards had replaced the days of making decisions for the parish with the help of two trustees. Back then, pastors had "assistants" to help with marriage prep and youth activities, and . . . run interference. And, of course, the pastors had always kept their own books.

It wasn't that Jack was in a complaining or self-pitying mood. No, he just couldn't ignore that so much had changed. Not only were the ranks thinner from departures, fewer ordinations, and the felt loss of religious, but the parishioners' expectations of the pastor were the same. Or maybe they were even greater, as parishioners compared models of leadership with their workplace experiences.

As he began the intercessions of evening prayer, it occurred to him that while it was natural to pray about the tragedies and successes of his people, about his temptations, about the loneliness and wonder he feels as a priest, about the polarizing struggles in the diocese and the universal Church, and about the many people suffering in wars and from hunger around the world, he couldn't remember the last time he prayed about the office work and the "administrative tasks" expected of him.

"Our Father. . . ." Just then the computer, which Irv had left online, stirred from its cyberworld slumber: "You've got mail!" ". . . and lead us not into temptation, but deliver us from . . . er . . . e-mail!" The prompter indicated it was from the bishop. "How did he get my e-mail address already?"

"*Curia eleison.*"

INTRODUCTION

All of this is pastoral life today, as I have learned from my own experience as a pastor and from a number of priests I spoke to before writing this essay. What do we see? Like Father Jack, priests are mostly satisfied with ministry. They know the support of their people; they are in good humor, and they demonstrate generous flexibility as they care for their people. But we also detect what one spiritual director terms a "low-level fever of dissatisfaction" in this otherwise healthy situation. More and more often, priests are expressing frustration about the ever-increasing administrative demands expected of them in parish ministry. Are these just the complaints of those who are averse to hard work or unwilling to adapt to new developments? Obviously the bishops thought not; some years ago, when writing on stress in ministry, they sympathetically recognized that such work leaves priests spiritually barren.[1] This dissatisfaction with administration deserves further attention, especially if we take for granted that administration is part of pastoral ministry. Even those pastors who dislike this work do not dispute this. There are just too many daily reminders that administration is part of our leadership role in our communities.

In order to better understand this dissatisfaction, we will first view it in the context of the rest of priestly ministry, which is otherwise satisfying. This will help us appreciate more fully what priests mean when they say such work leaves them disoriented, fatigued, and uneasy. We then can take up the question of how priests might approach administration differently, that is, in a way that links it to the rest of pastoral ministry that they find satisfying.

"FULL BUT FULFILLING DAYS"

Pastoral life is very rewarding for priests in spite of its many demands and their own limitations. The brief scene from Father Jack's life reveals that good pastoral care requires a significant personal commitment and an investment of time and energy. Priests consider it a worthwhile sacrifice. They see firsthand how Christ changes lives through their priestly service in word and sacrament. Those captivated by sin and selfishness are set free to be generous and forgiving as they come to know the Father's love. New disciples respond to the call of Christ to take up their crosses and follow him. Broken lives are healed and made whole by the same Spirit who raised Jesus from the dead.

The satisfaction priests enjoy in these areas of ministry is not merely a matter of self-fulfillment, a celebration of their own achievement, or a recognition of their initiatives meeting with success. They readily admit that their efforts are both imperfect and fragmentary. Their satisfaction comes, rather, in appreciating that Christ is working in them[2] to complete their otherwise wanting efforts. Their satisfaction involves delighting in the mystery that Christ makes their work his own by redeeming the little they have to make a significant and lasting contribution in the lives of the people they serve. This is how disciples have come to understand what it means to minister with Christ at their side, ever since the day when the Lord took from one of them a meager ration of loaves and fishes and used it to feed thousands. This satisfaction lies at the heart of our tradition of priestly ministry and prompts priests like Father Jack to speak of having a "full but fulfilling day."

"Spiritually Barren Work"

But priests also suffer from a "low-level fever of dissatisfaction" as they are expected to give more and more of their day to administrative duties. They often are left spiritually barren by such work. They describe it as feeling disoriented, fatigued, and uneasy.

Since Father Jack was ordained forty years ago, the world has become much more complex. We see these changes in society, in our culture, and in the Church. For instance, the pastor of today must respond to the growing accumulation of bureaucratic regulations such as zoning ordinances and health and safety codes, not to mention the accounting and employment standards issued by agencies of local, state, and federal governments. Of course, all of these new tasks require new and more sophisticated skills. In the past, Father Jack could pastor without being computer-literate, proficient in standard accounting and budgeting procedures, accomplished in techniques on collaboration, and so forth. All of these demands continue to multiply "to the degree that even relatively small parishes require technical and organizational leadership skills that are often very sophisticated."[3]

We also see how changes in the culture complicate pastors' efforts to lead and organize their parishes. Neighborhoods are constantly being reshaped into a more mobile society. This development has an impact upon parishes with more frequent turnovers in their membership rolls. Some priests report nearly a 30 percent rate of families rotating in and out of their parishes each year. Nontraditional families and diverse ethnic and racial groups in a given parish are also becoming the norm. For instance, a pastor of a large urban parish in the west recently noted that his community now represents eighteen different language groups. As a result of all of these changes, pastors cannot rely on the kind of stability or similarities that facilitated community building in the past. In fact, they must spend time and energy to develop new ways of promoting a sense of cohesion and belonging among otherwise unrelated groups of people.

Changes within the Church have also added to the pastor's lists of administrative tasks. It is taken for granted that priests are to be the agents of change in their parishes. Pastors have been and continue to be responsible for initiating and implementing the liturgical renewal, promoting greater lay participation, conforming to new diocesan regulations on a variety of levels, spearheading annual drives, and heightening awareness of political and social issues, to mention a few.

It is easy to see how all of this can leave priests disoriented. These demands come from all different directions, often making it difficult to know where to start. The old points of reference for how to lead a parish no longer seem to give direction in this new wilderness.

This disorientation turns into fatigue as priests begin to realize that the increase in the number and complexity of administrative tasks is a trend that in all likelihood will continue unabated each year. They also know from experience that even with fewer priests, people's expectations are the same or even greater. As one bishop recently noted, "The majority of Catholics have not yet understood how thin the ranks of priests are getting, and their expectations have not changed from twenty-five years ago." In fact, my own experience is that the expectations are even greater than in the past.

It is true that more and more parishes are hiring business managers for many administrative tasks. However, the pastor still is the one ultimately responsible to the Church to oversee so that the work is done competently. Also, to their credit, priests have taken up the challenge of developing new skills. They have benefited from diocesan workshops and seminars on these topics, as well as the kind of individual tutoring that parishioners like Irv seem to be giving Father Jack in getting him "online."

Nonetheless, priests are dissatisfied, feeling that all of this will never be quite enough. They are wearied by the prospect that more is yet to come, and they will never get caught up or measure up. Related to this is the perception that they have little or no say about additions to their "administrative job descriptions." As one priest told me, "Sometimes I think the only control left to me is not opening my mail," a tactic Father Jack seems to have learned quite well.

Priests also speak of feeling uneasy about this trend of giving more emphasis to administrative tasks. It seems to represent a shift in the priorities of ministry, a shift that is redefining that ministry. For instance, more and more they are being asked to set the sights of their people on pursuing palpable goals. How well they do in advancing such goals, then, becomes the standard for measuring a "successful parish" or a "successful pastor."

Many priests are uneasy about this for a number of reasons. First, their experience has taught them that quite often ministry done well has little to do with worldly success, and in fact, they would be considered unsuccessful or even a failure by the standards of the worldly success in much of what they do in caring for their people as pastors. Secondly, they fear that this continuing use of their "ministerial capital"—that is, their leadership and relationships with people—for such goals will eventually undermine their pastoral effectiveness. One pastor expressed this sentiment by noting that he believes he is making himself less spiritually available to some people in his parish because too many of his personal conversations with them are about money. In a word, he and many other priests fear that their ministry is being secularized.

Adam's message to Father Jack is a good example of how all of this can affect people's expectations of a pastor's leadership role. Basically, Adam is asking Father Jack to use his ministry of the word to help the stewardship committee target a certain group of fellow parishioners with the singular aim of increasing the number of financial pledges. Priests are particularly discouraged by this kind of misunderstanding, since it seems so disconnected from their own view of priesthood and the motivations that prompted and now sustain their vocation.

THE CHALLENGE

This brief overview helps us understand what priests are saying when they speak of their dissatisfaction with the increased emphasis on administration. First of all, these concerns should not be easily dismissed as the complaining of those who dislike hard work or are inflexible. As one bishop told me, "This dissatisfaction is having a real impact on our priests. Increasingly priests are talking about being tired. They are talking to each other about being tired. They also are talking about retiring as early as possible, and they are looking forward to it." Secondly, their dissatisfaction is best understood when we observe how it stands in marked contrast to the satisfaction they experience in the rest of ministry. This satisfaction comes in knowing that Christ is working in them and that his Spirit is in them. He is by their side to complete and redeem their limited efforts for the good of the people they serve. This is not the case with administrative work. Priests do not see the connection between the administration expected of them and the ministry they share with Christ. They are struggling with integrating these expectations with the rest of ministry, which is otherwise satisfying. This is what Father Jack is saying when he wonders why he does not include administrative tasks with the other pastoral concerns he brings to prayer.

Thirdly, we see that priests are struggling because administration in pastoral ministry is increasingly framed by the expectations, goals, and methods of secular society and the workplace models of success. We should not be surprised that this is happening. We live in a time when the world of business has seemingly perfected managerial strategies to guarantee success, which is so widely celebrated in our very materialistic culture. This tends to give such expectations an intimidating credibility, as though the world of business has been crowned the single voice competent to speak on such issues. The low-grade fever plaguing priests is the dissatisfaction that they can never meet these expectations, nor in many cases do they think they should even be trying.

All of this suggests, then, that pastoral administration needs to be framed differently, if it is to be integrated with the rest of ministry. Rather than defining it according to the expectations of secular society and the work place, we need to define it as work that is done with Christ's expectations of leadership. This means seeing our organizational and leadership efforts and aims as something we do in union with Christ, who makes our work his own. This redefining will also mean breaking free of the secular expectations of success that have such a powerful impact on our lives.

A good place to start is Jesus' description of his work in John 17, the Priestly Prayer of Jesus. There he gives an account of his work to the Father. He simultaneously reveals his expectations of those who continue this work in his name. Like him, they are to (1) work as those who are sent, (2) call disciples to know the Father, and (3) send these disciples out to complete this work.

The aim here will be to see how these expectations can be appropriated by priests in a way that transforms an approach to administration from one that now leaves them disoriented, fatigued, and uneasy, into one that gives them direction, strength, and hope.

ADMINISTRATION IN THE TRADITION OF JESUS

As One Sent

Jesus' self-description as "one sent by the Father" appears five times in John 17.[4] It is a title that most radically defines what it means for Jesus to be a servant. He does not come on his own initiative. He does not come to carry out his own wishes by responding to his own concerns or those of others that he decides are important. Rather, he takes his direction as one sent. Everything is from the Father. Jesus' priorities are the Father's priorities. Whatever he does is what he is sent to do.

As noted earlier, priests often lose their sense of direction and become disoriented by the increase and greater complexity of administrative tasks. These demands come from so many directions, making it impossible at times to know where to start. They feel the pressure of responding to the latest technological advances that promise to improve their administration and put it on the "cutting edge." New programs are portrayed as a "must-have" addition for a parish to be considered successful and up-to-date. This is not to say that these demands are unimportant, but they cannot set the direction for a pastor's ministry.

By taking on the mindset and priorities of Jesus for themselves, priests are reminded that they neither come on their own initiative, nor take direction solely from the circumstances they find in ministry. Someone like Father Jack is sensitive to the need to keep this understanding before him in the midst of a day that is overrun with many tasks. He does that by putting aside the messages. They can wait; his prayer cannot. That is because, as many priests have learned over time, prayer is the time amidst the day's activities wherein they recover their identity as those who are sent. This is where they rediscover their priorities, direction, and identity. As one spiritual director put it, "prayer is where Jesus tells us the truth about who we are, which is the only way we can redeem those false identities others try to give us in life." It is in prayer that we most fully appropriate what it means to serve as one sent.

To Call Disciples to Know the Father

This phrase succinctly summarizes the work the Father has sent Jesus to do. Anything Jesus receives from the Father—the power over all humanity, and the disciples whom the Father has taken from the world and given to him—is related to this purpose. He is to make the Father and the one who is sent by the Father known to the disciples. In doing so, Jesus is bringing them into the relationship he has with the Father. That is why Jesus says his work is to bring eternal life to his disciples.[5] The fatigue that priests experience in administration is not simply a matter of being physically spent from hard work. Rather, as described above, they are wearied by the fear that they will never get caught up or measure up to the expectations that continue to mushroom in number and complexity. Jesus' simple and uncomplicated portrayal of his work is a helpful reminder for priests in this regard. As with Jesus, the central work of a pastor is to bring the disciples entrusted to his care into communion with the Father and the Son, and with each other.[6] Building up this communion has always been the measure of a pastor's administrative leadership.[7] This will always be the expectation that will center pastors in the midst of a whirlwind of other claims on their time and energy.

The liturgy provides pastors with a unique moment each day to reclaim continually this understanding of the leadership they offer. The origin of the word "liturgy" itself suggests this, for *leitourgia* refers to public service exercised in the interest of the people as a whole. Liturgy done well will serve as the model for all other aspects of pastoral leadership because it will keep before the community and the pastor the singular aim of building up the communion of faith as the measure of all the work he does. It will also remind him that the strength he needs for his pastoral leadership, as with Jesus, comes in and for bringing people into this communion. Priests draw great strength in seeing people respond to the call of Christ with the same fervor that prompted their own vocation. One priest summed this sentiment up by telling me that "few things take the edge off of a tiring day like seeing someone responding to the call of the Gospel, and deciding that they are going to do good just because they have come to love God."

To Send These Disciples Out to Continue This Work
Even though Jesus speaks of having finished the work the Father gave him, there is still work to do. He asks the Father to consecrate his disciples as he sends them out to continue his work. They are to make the Father and the Son known to others, who will believe through the disciples' words. In fact, earlier Jesus offers the hopeful vision to the disciples that they will perform even greater works than his (Jn 14:12).

Here we find Jesus framing leadership in a way that runs counter to the expectations that priests often face today as administrators. These expectations define successful leadership in terms of finishing projects and attaining palpable goals and the personal recognition that accompanies them. Priests become uneasy with these expectations since they fear that pursuing them will secularize their ministry, with the result that they will eventually become less effective pastorally with their people. It is in this situation that priests are invited to look to Jesus, who readily admits that his work is unfinished and that its success lies in sending out disciples to continue and even enhance his work.

This means that a pastor offers leadership by commissioning others to share in the mission. This is not just a matter of sharing the workload to complete an isolated and tangible goal. Rather, by enlisting them in the mission a pastor reminds his people and himself that such work is part of their own consecration, their growth in holiness. This consecration in being sent out is the measure of success of a pastor, just as it was for Jesus in sending out the disciples to continue and enhance his work. Such an approach to administration and leadership undermines any attempt to measure success as finishing a project or attaining a palpable goal. It also provides a great deal of hope. The uncompleted tasks, instead of being judged as failures, become the work of those commissioned, who will do even greater things.

CONCLUDING REMARKS

Anyone writing on the priest as administrator today cannot ignore that pastors are becoming increasingly dissatisfied with this kind of work. From the way they talk about their frustrations, it is clear that they are finding it more difficult to identify the expectations of administration as part of pastoral ministry. Much of the administrative work in their pastoral life is often framed by the expectations of secular society and the workplace, which aim for measurable standards of success and the attainment of palpable goals.

The disorientation, fatigue, and uneasiness that priests experience in this situation are, therefore, indications that administration needs to be defined differently, if it is to be integrated into the rest of a ministry that is otherwise satisfying. That means defining the ministerial administration of a pastor as work that is done with Christ's expectations for leadership. In the face of disorientation, Jesus gives direction to a pastor by reminding him that he has been sent. Fatigued by the fear that he will never catch up or measure up to the demands made of him, a pastor hears Jesus recall for him that the measure of his work lies in calling disciples to know the Father. Building up the communion with the Father and the Son among the disciples gives him the strength he needs. Jesus also speaks to a pastor's uneasiness with the expectations that his leadership should aim for attaining palpable goals and be shaped by secular standards of success. When his experience tells him that much of his ministry is unsuccessful and unfinished, he finds hope by remembering that Jesus' work was finished by those whom he sent out—the measure of success for those who work with the expectations of Jesus.

The task of recovering our tradition of pastoral leadership does not belong solely to priests. Bishops and religious superiors can do much to reinforce these various aspects of a priest's identity. Clear communication with priests is essential here, especially when priorities are realigned and new directions are taken. When bishops and superiors include their priests in such discussions, they are reminding them of their mutual bonds to the common mission of the order or diocese. This inclusion is a way of affirming that they all share in this vocation of leadership and stewardship to make the Father known to the disciples so that they can be sent out. Rather than feeling left adrift in a wilderness of increasing new demands, pastors will look to this relationship of shared mission as the stabilizing point of reference to take up whatever new challenge the Church asks of them.

Bishops, religious superiors, and yes, lay people must all do their part in seeing that the administrative demands they make of their pastors find their point of reference in the tradition of Jesus' leadership rather than in the world of business or secular society. In that way, maybe the next time Father Jack celebrates vespers at the end of a long day, he will not hesitate to include his concerns about pastoral administration with all the other intentions he brings to his prayer.

NOTES

1   Cf. Bishops' Committee on Priestly Life and Ministry, National Conference of Catholic Bishops, *The Priest and Stress* (Washington, D.C.: United States Catholic Conference, 1982).

2   The New Testament refers to the presence of Christ in different ways. Johannine and Pauline texts speaking of an indwelling—such as "Christ living in me"—whereas the Synoptics more commonly portray the risen Christ at the side of the disciple, such as the Emmaus scene in Luke. I use both expressions alternately throughout this essay when speaking of the presence of Christ in the life and ministry of priests.

3   Bishops' Committee on Priestly Life and Ministry, National Conference of Catholic Bishops, *A Shepherd's Care: Reflections on the Changing Role of Pastor* (Washington, D.C.: United States Catholic Conference, 1987), p. 9.

4   Jesus repeatedly tells the Father in prayer that he does what he does because "*you sent me*," a phrase that appears in verses 8, 18, 21, 23, and 25. Cf. Raymond E. Brown, *The Gospel According to John: XIII-XXI*, vol. 29A, *The Anchor Bible* (Garden City, N.J.: Doubleday, 1970), p. 744.

5   As Raymond Brown notes in his commentary on this gospel text, "For John . . . knowing God is not a purely intellectual matter but involves a life of obedience to God's commandments and of loving communion with fellow Christians." Ibid., p. 752.

6   Properly understood, the primary meaning of *communio* "refers to our intimate relationship with the triune God. Communion is our participation in the life of the Spirit through faith, word and sacrament. . . . The secondary meaning . . . [refers to] the relationship among believers that is based on prior communion with God." Patrick Granfield, "The Concept of the Church as Communion," *Origins* 28:44 (April 22, 1999): 757.

7   The earliest reference to administration in our tradition is in 1 Corinthians 12:28. There Paul refers to *kubernasis*, "the ability to lead," as one of the *charismata*. By including administration in the list of gifts of the Spirit of Christ, he indicates its importance for the building up of the Body rather than for mere efficiency. *Kubernasis*, like gifts of healing (*iamaton*) and tongues (*glosson*) is given to certain members for the benefit and edification of all—of the Body.

TOWARD A FUTURE FULL OF HOPE: THE CHURCH CALLS FORTH PRIESTLY VOCATIONS FOR THE THIRD CHRISTIAN MILLENNIUM

Most Reverend Paul S. Loverde
Bishop of Arlington

Booker T. Washington once told the story about a sailing ship that had been lost for several weeks in the South Atlantic and had exhausted its supply of drinking water. Day after day, the vessel drifted beneath the merciless tropical sun. Then, after everyone had given up hope of being rescued, another ship came into view. The captain of the first ship sent out a signal: "We need fresh water." But the other ship signaled back, "Lower your buckets where you are."

The captain was certain that his message had been misunderstood, so he repeated the request: "We need fresh water." But the other ship sent back the same answer: "Lower your buckets where you are." Again the same message was sent, and again the same mysterious reply was received.

Finally, in desperation, the captain ordered his crew to lower their buckets over the side, and to their amazement, they drew up fresh water.

The lost ship had drifted near the coast of Brazil, and it was float-
ing on an immense stream of fresh water extending far out to sea
from the mouth of the Amazon River. The captain and his crew
had been dying of thirst while standing only a few feet away from
what they had been thirsting for. They were in a situation that
many of us also have experienced: they were aware of what they
needed, but they did not know where to look for it.

As priests, we know where to look for the priestly vocations needed in the third Christian millennium: We must look within the
Church and among ourselves. There was a time that we were in the
pews of our home parishes discerning a call to priesthood. In the
pews of our parishes is where the next generation of priests can be
found.

This is so clearly stated in *Pastores Dabo Vobis*, the apostolic
exhortation written by our Holy Father following the 1990 Synod
of Bishops. This synod focused on the increase of vocations to the
priesthood and the formation of priestly candidates. In chapter
four, "Come and See: Priestly Vocation in the Church's Pastoral
Work," our Holy Father refers to the Gospel of Saint John, chapter one, verses 35-42:

> The next day again John was standing with two of his dis-
> ciples; and he looked at Jesus as he walked, and said,
> "Behold, the Lamb of God!" The two disciples heard him
> say this, and they followed Jesus. Jesus turned, and saw
> them following, and said to them, "What do you seek?"
> And they said to him, "Rabbi" (which means Teacher),
> "where are you staying?" He said to them, "Come and
> see." They came and saw where he was staying; and they
> stayed with him that day, for it was about the tenth hour
> [four in the afternoon].

One of the two who heard John speak, and followed him, was Andrew, Simon Peter's brother. He first found his brother Simon, and said to him, "We have found the Messiah" (which means Christ). He brought him to Jesus. Jesus looked at him, and said, "So you are Simon the son of John? You shall be called Cephas" (which means Peter).[1]

Then the pope reminds us of the importance of pastoral work for vocations:

The Church gathers from this "*Gospel of vocation*" the paradigm, strength and impulse behind her pastoral work of promoting vocations, of her mission to care for the birth, discernment and fostering of vocations, particularly those to the priesthood. By the very fact that "the lack of priests is certainly a sad thing for any Church," pastoral work for vocations needs, especially today, to be taken up with a new vigor and more decisive commitment by all the members of the Church, in the awareness that it is not a secondary or marginal matter, or the business of one group only, as if it were a "part," no matter how important, of the entire pastoral work of the Church. Rather . . . it is an essential part of the overall pastoral work of each Church [diocese], a concern which demands to be integrated into and fully identified with the ordinary "care of souls," a connatural and essential dimension of the Church's pastoral work, of her very life and mission. Indeed, *concern for vocations is a connatural and essential dimension of the Church's pastoral work*.[2]

Our Holy Father is even more insistent on this point later in the apostolic exhortation:

The priestly vocation is a gift from God. It is undoubtedly a great good for the person who is its first recipient. But it is also a gift to the Church as a whole, a benefit to her life and mission. The Church, therefore, is called to safeguard this gift, to esteem it and love it. She is responsible for the birth and development of priestly vocations. Consequently, the pastoral work of promoting vocations has as its active agents, as its protagonists, the ecclesial community as such, in its various expressions: from the universal Church to the particular Church and, by analogy, from the particular Church to each of its parishes and to every part of the People of God.[3]

And, as he did earlier, the pope emphasizes this point again: "There is an urgent need, especially nowadays, for a more widespread and deeply felt conviction that *all the members of the Church, without exception, have the grace and responsibility to look after vocations.*"[4]

There is no doubt that the need for priests is great and real. This is true in our country. In 1965, there were 58,132 priests, whereas in 1999 there are 46,352—a loss of more than 10,000. Moreover, parishes without a resident priest have gone from 549 in 1965 to 2,617 in 1999. But in that same period of time, 1965-1999, the total number of Catholics has increased from 45.6 million to 59.2 million.[5]

While these statistics appear foreboding, there is much reason to be hopeful. Young people as well as older people seem more open to discerning God's call to priesthood (and also to the various forms of the consecrated life). The enthusiasm so evident in recent World Youth Days—in Denver, Manila, Paris, and Rome—points to a more favorable climate. So too do the results of recent research by the Center for Applied Research in the Apostolate (CARA). This research involved youth who actively participate in the life of the Church at the parish level, as well as their parents. Of this group, 6 percent indicated they have decided to pursue or are seriously thinking about pursuing a church vocation. Conservatively figured, this research estimates that each year more than 3,000 youths who are active in parish programs will pursue church vocations to the priesthood and to the consecrated life.[6]

I am amazed at how youth today gravitate to events that are identified as "extreme." "Extreme sports" such as bungee jumping or surfing out of airplanes seem to be the latest craze. "Extreme adventures" such as kayaking or mountain climbing seem to have even professionals like doctors and lawyers leaving the examination room or court room to grapple with Mother Nature.

I am convinced that we priests are called to "extreme discipleship." We cannot take lightly the call to obedience, celibacy, simplicity of life, fervent prayer, and humility. These may be difficult tasks at times, but they are our source of fulfillment. Our Holy Father refers to the "radical" nature of our vocation to priesthood.[7] I am delighted when our young people see these virtues lived out in dedicated and committed priests. And once again, we witness young people gravitating to these shepherds in order to ask their questions of faith, to seek the truth, and to find fulfillment in life.

A NATIONAL STRATEGY FOR THE PASTORAL WORK OF VOCATIONS

An increased interest and enthusiasm seem evident among those young people who are already active in the Church. Aware of these present realities, and mindful that all in the Church must collaborate in the work of vocations, the United States bishops unanimously endorsed a three-year national strategy for vocations entitled *A Future Full of Hope* (1996-1998).[8]

The national strategy was a definite response to Pope John Paul II's repeated emphasis that the pastoral work of vocations is truly the responsibility of everyone in the Church and that, therefore, everyone's involvement is needed. Moreover, the national strategy responded to the increased enthusiasm and interest among a good number of our youth and made available many positive approaches already experienced within some dioceses and religious communities in our country. From my perspective, this national strategy was a concrete expression of partnership, solidarity, and collaboration in the pastoral work of vocations. It sought to engage within the Church responsibility that is interconnected, interdependent, and collaborative in a variety of ways, through and with many groups—all this in a harmonious manner. For example, the ways in which this pastoral work became implemented were indeed varied:

- Through prayer: the *sine qua non* ingredient, to which we shall return later
- By targeting various age groups: from grade school through high school and college, and into graduate school and the workplace
- On many levels: parish, deanery, diocesan, provincial, regional, and national

A number of groups willingly pledged themselves to this national strategy, including the National Council of Catholic Women, Serra International, and the Knights of Columbus.

Obviously, it is important not only to identify but also to pursue potential vocations. This can be done in a concrete and productive manner by using feeder systems that have been developed in recent years. Such feeder systems include the Ministry Potential Discerner and The Story of My Soul.

The goals outlined in the strategy provide an excellent summary:

1. To foster a national campaign of prayer asking God for an increase of vocations to the priesthood and the religious life (Mt 9:38)

2. To engage more men and women in the vocation discernment process through national and local programs of education, invitation, recruitment and testing

3. To foster the role of "inviter" as a privilege and responsibility that belongs to each member of the Body of Christ in encouraging others to consider priesthood, religious life and secular institutes

4. To promote collaboration among bishops, diocesan priests, religious, and lay organizations on diocesan, regional and national levels in the area of vocational pastoral ministry

5. To encourage parish communities and their individual members to accept their responsibility for encouraging and calling forth vocations

6. To recommend quality educational programs and enrichment opportunities for vocation ministers

7. To engage in vocational pastoral ministry through promotion and education which will significantly broaden the base of those contacted and invited to consider priesthood and religious life, and expand those lay organizations, such as Serra, directly involved in vocation recruitment in the United States

8. To endorse and create vocation awareness and educational materials/tools/media which convey a contemporary, positive image of priesthood and religious life (e.g., in cooperation with the National Coalition for Church Vocations)

9. To direct vocation awareness and invitation to specific audiences—(a) families, (b) parishes, (c) campuses, (d) communities of color, (e) rural areas, (f) apostolic groups and organizations
10. To engage priests to encourage and invite young people to consider priesthood and religious life[9]

The national strategy was therefore understood as "a proactive, visionary program to reaffirm the priesthood and consecrated life as vibrant and life-giving callings; to educate the entire Church in the most modern, effective means of vocation ministry; to call forth, for the first time ever, a united, collaborative vocational effort on a nationwide scale; and to recognize the deep-seated calls to virtue, holiness and service that continue to exist in men and women today."[10]

The principles of this national strategy remain solid and continue to operate even though the formal three-year period has ended. The core of the national strategy is the implementation that takes place at the local level of the diocese—and, within the diocese, at the level of the parish. It is at this local or foundational level that vocations to the priesthood are best fostered. While the diocesan bishop is key to this process at the local level, no one person can do this work by himself. Thus, the national strategy calls for the collaboration of others with the bishop in this vital pastoral work. Closest to him in this work are diocesan and religious vocation directors.

Within the areas of communications, much has been and continues to be accomplished at both the local and national level. Dioceses and parishes have been successful in engaging the local media to carry positive stories of seminarians and of newly ordained priests. Aware that many people in our society, especially our youth, surf the Internet, a number of dioceses and parishes are developing websites that have a vocation link. This can offer the inquirer a whole range of vocation-oriented data. Through the Department of Communications of the United States Catholic Conference, kits featuring vocations were developed and later distributed at two national gatherings of the Catholic press. These kits contain useful information on vocations, including summaries of the recent research sponsored by the Bishops' Committee on Vocations.

PASTORAL WORK FOR VOCATIONS ON THE LOCAL LEVEL

Implications of the research undertaken through CARA and funded by Serra are truly important, especially at the local level:

1. Since the research indicates that young people involved with the Church are more likely to consider a church vocation, we need to involve our youth in parish life and to appeal to their idealism and enthusiasm. Thus, for example, we need to expand their presence among lectors, servers, and those who lead the Prayers of the Faithful.

2. Since priests and religious continue to play an indispensable role in vocations, they need to be encouraged and enabled to become more active "inviters." Conversations may be needed individually or as a presbyterate or congregation to address and resolve their hesitation and reluctance to invite.

3. Since parents can help to provide an environment conducive to vocations, they need to be encouraged to provide such an atmosphere, but at the same time, their questions and concerns need to be heard and discussed.

4. Since celibacy is not as much of an obstacle for those seriously considering a vocation as it is for youth in general, rather than apologize for celibacy, we need to foster a genuine witness to celibacy and provide a clear rationale, while addressing the misconceptions of celibacy in the media.[11]

Returning to the gospel event I cited earlier, the call of the first disciples as recorded in John 1:35-42, I ask you to recall that Andrew went home and then brought his brother Simon to Jesus. Our Holy Father comments, "This passage of John, which is also significant for the Christian vocation as such, has a particular value with regard to the priestly vocation. As the community of Jesus' disciples, the Church is called to contemplate this scene which in some way is renewed constantly down the ages."[12]

Yes, this scene is repeated again and again in parishes within this country, as individuals—such as a priest, parent, friend, teacher, parishioner—invite a man to consider God's call to the priesthood. Often, the context for this invitation can be programs like Called by Name or Operation Andrew. Some dioceses are reporting significant success with these programs. Teen retreats can also provide a favorable environment in order for this "invitation" to be given and heard. In fact, recent research has shown that many of the youths surveyed—52 percent—predicted that confirmation retreats focused on vocation could be very effective in encouraging affirmative responses to discerning God's call.[13]

The mysteries of faith that we celebrate bring youth in touch with the realization that there is more to life and love than what is presented to them in society. Efforts to put youth in touch with these mysteries can be seen in various youth retreats and the celebration of the sacraments. Youth groups that take the opportunity to pray the rosary and meditate on the joyful, sorrowful, and glorious mysteries experience a heightened level of involvement in the Church.

The mystery and power of the proclaimed word is something that captures youth. A simple word can have a significant impact. An example of this is the difference of a child who is verbally battered and one who is lovingly supported. Isaiah says, "Speak to the weary a word that will rouse them" (cf. Is 50:4). To give to God's young people the word—a gift that will give them hope and strength during their life—is a wonderful mystery to celebrate. As priests and as God's faithful people, we take the mystery of the Word made flesh very seriously. We continue to watch this mystery unfold in our own lives as we persevere in proclaiming it. Touched by this word, we are changed.

Our Holy Father reminds us,

> *"Live the mystery that has been placed in your hands!"* This is the invitation and admonition which the Church addresses to the priest in the Rite of Ordination, when the offerings of the holy people for the Eucharistic Sacrifice are placed in his hands. The "mystery" of which the priest is a "steward" (cf. 1 Cor 4:1) is definitively Jesus Christ himself, who in the Spirit is the source of holiness and the call to sanctification. This "mystery" seeks expression in the priestly life. For this to be so, there is need for great vigilance and lively awareness. Once again, the Rite of Ordination introduces these words with this recommendation: "be aware of what you will be doing." In the same way that Paul had admonished Timothy, "Do not neglect the gift you have" (1 Tm 4:14; cf. 2 Tm 1:6).[14]

In 1947, when I was a child in Connecticut, a cousin of mine from the Buffalo diocese was ordained to the priesthood. He came to visit with my family, and I recall that there was something about him that just touched me. I can't put it into words, but I remember saying to Mom and Dad at the age of eight or nine that I wanted to be like Fr. Mike when I grew up. I recall also thinking in those earlier years about being a lawyer, a teacher, or a christian brother—but in the end, I wanted to be a priest. To manifest to God's people the mysteries that are so much a part of our faith—there is an excitement in living out such a vocation. The Congregation for the Clergy puts it this way: "Configuration to Christ in sacramental ordination places the priest at the heart of God's people."[15]

It is important that a priest

> take particular care concerning vocations, encouraging prayer for vocations, doing his best in the work of catechetics, and taking care of the formation of the ministers. He will promote appropriate initiatives through a personal rapport with those under his care, allowing him to discover their talents and to single out the will of God for them, permitting a courageous choice in following Christ. . . . It would be desirable that every priest be concerned with inspiring at least one priestly vocation which could thus continue the ministry.[16]

It is our responsibility to regenerate the priesthood. I recall a beautiful passage from the Holy Father's letter to his priests on Holy Thursday, 1983. He states,

> "No longer do I call you servants . . . but I have called you friends." It was precisely in the Upper Room that those words were spoken, in the immediate context of the institution of the Eucharist and of the ministerial priesthood. Christ made known to the Apostles, and to all those who inherit from them the ordained Priesthood, that in this vocation and for this ministry they must become His friends—they must become the friends of that mystery which He came to accomplish. To be a priest means to enjoy special friendship with the mystery of Christ, with the mystery of the Redemption, in which He gives his flesh "for the life of the world."[17]

When all is said and done, the most effective arena for promoting, identifying, and calling forth vocations is the parish. It is to this arena that I now turn our attention. Our Holy Father states, "The indispensable role of the priest within the community must lead all the members of the Church in America to recognize the importance of promoting vocations. . . . Vocations 'are a gift of God' and 'they are born in communities of faith, above all in the family, the parish, Catholic schools and other Church organizations.'"[18]

Prayer
First and foremost is the centrality of prayer: individuals and families, as well as bishops, clergy, and religious, begging "the [Lord] of the harvest to send out laborers for his harvest" (Mt 9:38). Our Holy Father reminds us, "The Church, in her dignity and responsibility as a priestly people, possesses in prayer and in the celebration of the *Liturgy the essential and primary stages of her pastoral work for vocations.*"[19] Let us ponder this *sine qua non* from a variety of viewpoints.

1. We priests must encourage individuals and families within the parish to ask in prayer that the Lord will choose someone from their families to serve as a priest. Our Holy Father indicates this so emphatically in *Vita Consecrata*:

> I address you, Christian families. Parents, give thanks to the Lord if he has called one of your children to the consecrated life. It is to be considered a great honor— as it always has been—that the Lord should look upon a family and choose to invite one of its members to set out on the path of the evangelical counsels! Cherish the desire to give the Lord one of your children so that

God's love can spread in the world. What fruit of conjugal love could be more beautiful than this? . . . I pray that you, Christian families, united with the Lord through prayer and the sacramental life, will create homes where vocations are welcomed.[20]

Yes, each parish within this nation must become a powerhouse of prayer. We are finding—"rediscovering" is a better word—that prayer before our Lord eucharistically present is especially powerful in calling forth and sustaining priestly vocations. Marian devotions, too—especially the rosary, whereby we ask the help of Mary, Mother of Christ and Mother of the Church—cannot but strengthen our unceasing prayer: "Send us, O Lord, faithful and holy priests, shepherds after the Heart of Jesus!"

2. Not only is personal and family prayer so indispensable to the pastoral work of vocations, but so is liturgical prayer. Our Holy Father turns our attention to this in *Pastores Dabo Vobis*:

> The Liturgy, as the summit and source of the Church's existence and in particular of all Christian prayer, plays an influential and indispensable role in the pastoral work of promoting vocations. The Liturgy is a living experience of God's gift and a great school for learning how to respond to his call. As such, every liturgical celebration, and especially the Eucharist, reveals to us the true face of God and grants us a share in the Paschal Mystery. . . .[21]

3. Moreover, we need to encourage potential candidates for the priesthood, both young and not so young, to pray. Our Holy Father describes this so attractively and compellingly in *Pastores Dabo Vobis*:

> Indeed, Christian prayer, nourished by the word of God, creates an ideal environment where each individual can discover the truth of his own being and the identity of the personal and unrepeatable life project which the Father entrusts to him. It is therefore necessary to educate boys and young men so that they will become faithful to prayer and meditation on God's word: in silence and listening, they will be able to perceive the Lord who is calling them to the priesthood, and be able to follow that call promptly and generously.[22]

Think of the implications of this call to prayer within the family circle, our Catholic schools and CCD programs, college campuses, and ministry to young adults! While prayer is not the only thing we must do in identifying, calling forth, and nurturing priestly vocations, it is the first and most necessary. Yes, there is no doubt that the foundation of all pastoral work for vocations lies in prayer: our response to the Lord who urges us to prayer unceasingly for more laborers in his harvest field.

Vocations Committees

Yet another arena for parish involvement is the establishment of vocations committees, often under the umbrella of the parish pastoral council. Usually small in number, these few but hardworking parishioners can make the whole parish community more "vocation-conscious." Under the direction of the pastor, this committee can serve as the catalyst for the following:

- Creatively planning ways whereby those being called by God might be invited to consider a vocation
- Encouraging those who have already accepted an invitation to persevere
- Praying themselves and encouraging others to pray, especially parents

Moreover, such a committee, united with the pastor, can serve as a link between the diocesan bishop and his collaborators and the rest of the parish. A number of dioceses are reporting much benefit from this type of committee.

The Witness of Priests and Consecrated Persons

What is so key is the involvement of the clergy, religious, and laity who form each parish. As I mentioned above, parents need to be enabled to understand the wonder of a vocation occurring in their family and to be encouraged to pray for and support the vocation from within the family circle or "domestic Church." Often, they have serious questions and concerns that must be addressed as honestly, compassionately, and completely as possible. Surely the joy-filled positive witness of priests and consecrated persons will likewise be powerful in inviting those called to hear and to respond and in encouraging parents and family members to be supportive.

In terms of priestly vocations, what is truly crucial is the attitude of our priests, both diocesan and religious. Recent research reveals that only 18 percent of the youth surveyed have been personally encouraged by a priest, sister, or brother to consider a church vocation.[23] As earlier research—the *National Vocations Strategy Background Synthesis* of the NCCB Committee on Vocations—points out, during the 1960s, unfortunately the percentage of diocesan priests who actively encouraged boys to enter the seminary dropped from

64 percent to 33 percent and for religious priests from 56 percent to 27 percent.[24] These figures have not changed over the last three decades. The *Background Synthesis* puts it quite clearly:

> It is impossible to emphasize enough the importance of personal witness on the part of priests and religious to personally share the viability of the commitment they have made with others.[25]

> When priests invite young men to consider the priesthood in a personal, meaningful way, vocations are sparked. When they don't, very little else will work. . . . Invitations to religious life as a sister, brother, or priest also depend on personal invitation. . . .[26]

In the face of the seeming hesitation/reluctance on the part of priests to call forth vocations, much needs to be done. For example, dialogue is needed not only to clarify what are the underlying reasons but also to reaffirm the wonder of the priestly vocation, its vital impact on the lives of God's people, and its essential place alongside other vocations and other forms of church ministry. Several years ago, studies indicated that priests are happy and content in their work. We as priests must reflect this in ways that are tangible, so that our personal witness can attract and stimulate positive responses to God, who is now calling others to the priesthood even as he did us in the past. Moreover, the relationship of each diocesan bishop with his priests is also so influential in creating a deepening mutual cooperation on this issue.

It is so clear that all of us who are called by God to the pastoral work of vocations, and especially priests, need to be transformed through prayer so that ours is the mind, the attitude, the desire of Jesus himself. He so thirsted that God's love for his people would be known and accepted, understood and embraced—in a word, experienced—so that they could really live: "I came so that they might have life and have it more abundantly" (Jn 10:10). "This is eternal life, that they should know you, the only true God, and the one whom you sent, Jesus Christ" (Jn 17:3). Jesus was passionate about proclaiming the Good News of God's love—the core of the "New Evangelization": "I have come to set the earth on fire, and how I wish it were already blazing!" (Lk 12:49). Are we, as priests of God's people, impassioned like Jesus to proclaim the Good News who is Christ, Lord and Savior? Are we priests on fire with love for God and for the people entrusted by him to our pastoral care? Are we priests eager that the word be preached, that the sacraments be celebrated (especially the Eucharistic Sacrifice and sacrament of Penance), that leadership be given, that the various charisms and ministries be accepted and lived? Do we priests in a particular way desire that we be collaborators with the Lord, instruments in his name, as he calls forth men to the sacred priest-hood and both men and women to consecrated life? Yes, are we all truly seeking to be ecclesial: persons of obedient faith, guided by the Scripture, the tradition of the Church, and the teaching office of the Church, in exercising the pastoral work of vocations? In all this, our attitude is so crucial, and the only attitude we must have is that of Christ Jesus. For that, we must be rooted in him and transformed by prayerful union with him!

Insistently and consistently, our Holy Father has invited us to participate in the new evangelization. Is not the pastoral work for vocations closely linked with this new evangelization? After all, in bringing Christ to every sphere of human activity through the witness and involvement of dedicated committed lay persons, priests will be needed to proclaim the word, to celebrate the sacraments, and to give guidance and direction. Through their ministry, those who believe can be deepened in their life of faith; those who struggle may be drawn to the Source of Light and Truth and Love, and those who are not yet believers may be brought to him who alone is the Way, the Truth, and the Life. As the new evangelization leads to the deepening of faith on the part of young people and enables them to respond with enthusiasm and vigor to the Christian vocation to holiness and service, a new wave of vocations to priesthood and consecrated life will surely surface.

The principal agent in the new evangelization is God the Holy Spirit; so is he in the pastoral work for vocations. Our Holy Father himself states, "At the conclusion of the [1990] Synod, I said that in the face of a crisis of priestly vocations 'the first answer which the Church gives lies in a total act of faith in the Holy Spirit. We are deeply convinced that this trusting abandonment will not disappoint if we remain faithful to the graces we have received.'"[27]

Allow me to conclude with a favorite image of mine. Remember, when we were children, how fascinated we were to watch what happened when we threw a pebble into a pool of water! We saw ripples, and when several of us threw pebbles in at the same time, we were amazed at how the criss-crossing ripples became so many centers of energy that, in fact, moved the pool's water!

You and I—all in the Church—are like so many sources of energy directed by the Holy Spirit. When we freely and generously give of our very selves to the pastoral work for vocations—like throwing pebbles into the pool—will not new and energizing currents be released, attracting potential candidates to respond to God's call? Will not a future full of hope be created and sustained within this great Church in the United States as we enter the third Christian millennium?

1 Cited in John Paul II, *Pastores Dabo Vobis* (PDV) (*I Will Give You Shepherds*) (Washington, D.C.: United States Catholic Conference, 1992), no. 34.

2 Ibid.

3 Ibid., no. 41.

4 Ibid.

5 These comparisons use statistics from selected volumes of *The Official Catholic Directory* (New Providence, N.J.: P. J. Kenedy and Sons, 1886-2000).

6 Bishops' Committee on Vocations, National Conference of Catholic Bishops, *Survey of Catholic Youth and Parents Connected with Parish Programs: Findings and Implications for Vocations* (Washington, D.C.: Center for Applied Research in the Apostolate, Georgetown University, June 1997), p. 35.

7 Cf. PDV, no. 17.

8 Bishops' Committee on Vocations, National Conference of Catholic Bishops, *A Future Full of Hope: The U.S. Bishops' National Vocation Strategy, 1996-1998* (Washington, D.C.: NCCB Committee on Vocations, 1996).

9 Ibid., pp. 3-4.

10 Ibid., p. 2.

11 Paul S. Loverde, presentation at NCCB General Meeting, June 1997. Based on the *Survey of Youth and Parents Connected with Parish Programs*, op. cit., pp. 1-3.

12 PDV, no. 34.

13 *Survey of Youth and Parents Connected with Parish Programs*, op. cit., p. 30.

14 PDV, no. 24.

15 Congregation for the Clergy, *The Priest and the Third Christian Millennium: Teacher of the Word, Minister of the Sacraments, and Leader of the Community* (Washington, D.C.: United States Catholic Conference, 1999), chapter 3, no. 1.

16 Congregation for the Clergy, *Directory on the Ministry and Life of Priests* (Vatican City: Libreria Editrice Vaticana, 1994), no. 34.

17 John Paul II, Holy Thursday Letter to Priests, 1983.

18 John Paul II, *Ecclesia in America (The Church in America)* (Washington, D.C.: United States Catholic Conference, 1999), no. 40.

19 PDV, no. 38.

20 John Paul II, *Vita Consecrata (The Consecrated Life)* (Washington, D.C.: United States Catholic Conference, 1996), no. 107.

21 PDV, no. 38.

22 Ibid.

23 *Survey of Youth and Parents Connected with Parish Programs*, op. cit., p. 36.

24 Bishops' Committee on Vocations, National Conference of Catholic Bishops, *National Vocations Strategy Background Synthesis* (Washington, D.C.: Center for Applied Research in the Apostolate, Georgetown University, February 1997), p. 5.

25 Ibid., p. 6.

26 Ibid., p. 5.

27 PDV, no. 11.

.